50¢

MW00910572

Paths to Prayer

Jesus' Appearance after the Resurrection
First Baptist Church of Charlotte, Charlotte, North Carolina

Paths to Prayer

A Little Book of
New Testament Devotions

Lore Kephart

Providence House Publishers
PROVIDENCE PUBLISHING CORPORATION
FRANKLIN, TENNESSEE

Printed in the United States of America

08   07   06   05   04   1   2   3   4   5

Library of Congress Control Number: 2004097366

Includes fourteen color plates.

ISBN: 1-57736-328-0

Scripture references are from the Life Application Bible, New Revised Standard Version of the Bible, copyright 1989 by the Division of Christian Education of the National Council of the Churches of Christ in the USA. Used by permission. All rights reserved.

Photo on cover and page 37 used courtesy of Henry Weis and photo on page 104 used courtesy of Tom Young.

Cover design by Hope Seth

Published in conjunction with Bookscape Publishing, Inc.

PROVIDENCE HOUSE PUBLISHERS
an imprint of
Providence Publishing Corporation
238 Seaboard Lane • Franklin, Tennessee 37067
www.providence-publishing.com
800-321-5692

To Jeremy, Miranda, Julia, Owen, Daniel, and Claire—
very grand grandchildren!

Contents

Preface

It would be true enough to say that this book of devotions was an outgrowth of my Great Decisions work over the last eighteen years, an interest group which is an integral part of Presbyterian Women of the Bryn Mawr Presbyterian Church in Bryn Mawr, Pennsylvania. Great Decisions discussion groups are the right arm of the Foreign Policy Association in New York. These groups number in the hundreds and are located throughout the United States; their purpose is to present a forum for untangling the web of international problems which saturate our planet. Terrorism, problems in the Middle East, and the European Union are among the inescapable issues we tackle.

Somewhere along the way, I began putting the devotions and themes I offered before each lecture into little booklets, never expecting them to reach beyond the periphery of this wonderful group of people. But I kept receiving requests for "just another copy" until I realized there might be meaning for others within those covers.

The truth, however, is that I will never be convinced that I would have had the intense commitment to Great Decisions had I not grown up believing that I had a personal mission to do as Jesus would have me do. This was instilled in me many years ago by my mother, her everfaithful friends, and Sunday School teachers who guided me along the path of Bible stories,

Bible drills, memorization, activities, and—more than anything—the quiet, exemplary way they lived their lives. Teachers who taught us to be "kind and true" were themselves. All this came from my home church, Southwestern Presbyterian Church in Southwest Philadelphia.

Then it became my turn! When I was fifteen, I began teaching Sunday School, an avocation which came to have several mutations: superintendent of the Primary department and assistant junior high coordinator at a downtown Wilmington, Delaware church we joined after I was married; and even a time when my husband and I served as senior high counselors at a Methodist church we attended.

As children at Southwestern Presbyterian Church's Beginners' Department, our class lustily sang this song:

Red and yellow, black and white;
They are precious in his sight;
Jesus loves the little children of the world.

Here we have the words of a childhood song ultimately manifesting itself in my unqualified interest in the world around me and my ensuing dedication to helping others understand, as best I can, the inherent problems people of every race and culture encounter. It is my desire that this book lead to discussions that would generate an interest in some specific problem which could reverberate in a helpful way.

This has been a strenuous journey, but it has been pursued ardently and with much care. In the beginning, it seemed to me that the compatibility of words and color presented in this particular way would be another step toward understanding Christian beliefs taught to me long ago. Now I know I was clearly being beckoned ever-so-gently along a path leading me ever closer to heavenly light.

Lore Kephart
August 2004

Acknowledgments

I mean to praise those whose names follow, for each one has made a singularly unique contribution to this book: Gina Dyer, moderator of Presbyterian Women (2002–2003) for her unexpected encouragement while officiating at her last board meeting in challenging me to publish my prayer books; Margaret Anne Fohl, associate pastor, Pastoral Care, Bryn Mawr Presbyterian Church, who did not hesitate to take on the task of reading through my manuscript when I asked her. She lifted a substantial burden from me in the doing; Rev. Adrian Gilligan, O.S.A., for introducing me to the work of William Barclay, the backbone of my efforts herein; Loretta Smith, my lifetime friend, who happens to be a gifted grammarian and professor, and who also knows the art of giving a friend a gentle push; and Diana Rossi for her gift of friendship and my cherished Bible.

A sincere thank you to the staff at Willet Stained Glass Studios for their professional and knowledgable assistance. They include Corwin Smith, research librarian, who carefully and patiently scanned our choices; Elaine Johnson-Spivey, receptionist/secretary for her courtesy and help; Susan Wing, art historian, who helped in our search for appropriate illustrations; and Helene Weis, senior librarian, who found essential illustrations for us and is noted throughout the stained glass community for her seemingly unequaled knowledge of stained glass. Valuable source material for the stained glass primer furnished by the Stained Glass Association of America and Art Glass Association was particularly appreciated. Mention must be made of Nancy Wise, managing editor, for her patience and competence in guiding this rather complicated manuscript into homeport; Hope Seth, for her wonderful and refreshing design of this book; Mike VanHook, director of business development and marketing, for his knowledgable help in opening the doors of publishing to me; and Tammy Spurlock and Kelli Wallace for their hard work and attention to detail.

Our children—Jeff, Beth, and Janice—have made our lives fulfilling because of their consistent and individual successes. This has been a natural form of inspiration. My husband, Kep (formally known as Horace L. Kephart), had a keen sense of seeing what he could do in order to move this manuscript along—and always did it. He has mastered the high art of encouragement, often mending my spirits on a moment's notice. This has rounded out to near-perfect love and living, for which I offer him immeasurable thanks.

A Tribute to E. Crosby Willet

O nce the decision was made to publish this book, the idea for its cover was only a heartbeat away, for I had some hand in designing the 8' x 8' Willet stained glass window which was installed in Southwestern Presbyterian Church in honor of my mother and brother in 1992. I wish you could see its illuminated beauty "in person."

Seldom are family businesses carried on by subsequent generations with the enthusiasm that E. Crosby Willet, grandson of the founder of Willet Stained Glass Studios and its longtime president, has retained. A sprinkling of the awards he has received from organizations include the American Stained Glass Association for his major influence in this noble field. More recently, he was the recipient of the Elbert M. Conover Memorial Award from the Interfaith Forum on Religion, Art, and Architecture which honors non-architects for distinguished contributions in stained glass.

I met Crosby in 1991 when my husband and I decided to make a gift of a Willet stained glass window to Southwestern Presbyterian Church in southwest Philadelphia, my childhood church. The man's love for what he was doing was immediately apparent in his creative involvement. I can claim some credit for its design, but I wanted the cross to be the window's centerpiece. It was just "there" until Crosby suggested beveling the ruby glass I had chosen, which would produce a natural gold edging, thereby giving the cross a definitive golden glow. It was a masterstroke!

A competitor of Tiffany in the first decades of the twentieth century, the Willet Stained Glass Studios began manufacturing windows in 1898. With their reputation for beauty and durability untarnished, the studios continue designing and manufacturing stained glass windows in their Germantown, Philadelphia, facility. Although you may not have realized it, if you have visited West Point, Princeton University, the National Cathedral, or any of thousands of churches, hospitals, cemeteries, or universities here or abroad, you have been in the light of a Willet window.

I had the pleasure of visiting with Crosby recently, and I asked him what it was about his lifelong work which has kept his interest so heightened. After a considered moment, for Crosby considers everything, he replied, "their beauty."

Although Willet stained glass windows have graced count-less publications throughout their more-than-a-century history, I am honored that this little book represents the first time Willet windows have been featured exclusively. Noting the thousands of Willet windows produced through the years, careful research may reveal that your own place of worship may, in fact, house a prized Willet window(s).

In any case, I am certain that you will agree that E. Crosby Willet's uncluttered response to the question posed him above is anything but an exaggeration of this enduring and elegant artform.

A Stained Glass Primer

*I*t has been written of Abbot Suger (1122–1151 A.D.) of France's Abbey of St. Denis that, "He truly believed that the presence of beautiful objects would lift men's souls closer to God."

While one of my dictionaries states that stained glass is, in part, "glass that has been colored, enameled, or painted," a more aesthetic definition refers to it as "the transformation of the ordinary into the mystical."

Most of us understand the latter definition because of what our hearts tell us, but let us put that theory into practice. Recently, I participated in our Presbyterian Women's annual Spirituality Day. We were encouraged to think about what was most likely to put us in a prayerful mood. Music and scripture were mentioned, but one woman volunteered that, although she found it difficult to explain, the changing light and color coming from stained glass windows affected her visually as well as emotionally, i.e., they were the catalysts for her most prayerful moments.

Following is a cursory history of the advent of glass; then we will return to that which is more meaningful for us: the more sacred elements.

The use of the earliest man-made glass dates back beyond the second century B.C. to what is known today as the Middle East, most notably in Egypt. While Romans are credited with incorporating glass into windows in the first century A.D., the use of colored glass can be dated from around the seventh century A.D., where it was found in an English monastery. (Color in stained glass derives from the addition of specific metal oxides; for example, copper and cobalt render green and blue.) Centuries later, as Gothic churches came into prominence, stained glass became their natural accompaniment when Renaissance influences became the persuasive thinking of the times (c. mid-fifteenth century until the end of the sixteenth century). It became popular again with the Gothic revival that began in the late eighteenth century.

Then, in the late nineteenth century, the Bolton brothers from England opened the first glass studio in America. Other studios, such as Willet (established in 1898), were also ready for this reawakening. Additional energy for creating stained glass windows in this country emerged around the same time, when John LaFarge and Louis Comfort Tiffany, contemporary competitors, introduced a new type of glass which they called opalescent, a milky kind of glass with an iridescent appearance. An innovation in the twentieth century was that of faceted or chipped glass which is set into concrete or epoxy resin.

What are the more sacred highlights? It is fitting that one of the most integral parts of churches and church life—stained glass—is attributable to no one in particular and its proliferation to many. But there was, as we shall see, a certain impetus for this movement, a contribution attributable to none other than the Abbot Suger, introduced above, and a twelfth century German monk, Theophilus.

Over the centuries, the use of stained glass multiplied. Sanctuaries of every kind—abbeys, basilicas, cathedrals, and monasteries—all began to incorporate the light and color stained glass so generously offers. Small, mosaic-like windows were gradually replaced with more detailed and compelling religious subjects, as the unique properties of stained glass became ever-more appreciated. Gothic-style churches, described as "religious in inspiration and ecclesiastical in nature" were being built all over Europe—Spain, Germany, France, England, etc.

First, we must pay tribute to the German monk, Theophilus, who, in his twelfth century "A Treatise Upon Various Arts," described with great detail the art of "composing" glass windows. His instructions remain to this time an imposing reference point for stained glass craftsmen.

It was also in the twelfth century that Gothic architecture and stained glass became mystical, impermeable partners, when in 1122, the "remarkable" Abbot Suger began reforming the abbey church of St. Denis near Paris. In their landmark book, *Stained Glass* (a must for anyone with the vaguest interest in stained glass), authors Lawrence Lee, George Seddon, and Francis Stephens describe Suger as the "father of Gothic architecture," for it was in 1144 that "Suger's beautiful creation, the abbey church of St. Denis, was consecrated." Personally arranging for the design of many of the stained glass windows, he was not troubled by any perceived ostentation, for he was determined "to illumine men's minds so that they may travel through it to an apprehension of God's light."

Until the sixteenth century, Gothic-style churches remained the greatest inspiration in the building of religious dwellings. The Cologne Cathedral, built in 1248 in Germany, for example, took decades to complete and became the largest Gothic church in Europe. Gothic churches, however, experienced a decline, as did the style of stained glass windows they so gloriously housed. Many churches, along with their windows, were destroyed. By the nineteenth century, however, architects were again insisting upon the return of the Gothic style and, of course, stained glass with them.

Given its resilient history, it is not difficult to accept that "stained glass is the only art in the service of Christian worship wholly developed during the Christian era." It is, therefore, my great hope that this book will encourage you to let your faith act as your host to ecclesiastic history by visiting churches of every denomination when you travel. Many churches throughout our country are properly aware of their history and the inspiration stained glass windows in their church will forever be. Some have even established Internet sites designed to encourage you to travel to their locations. There is much to be inspired by, learned, and savored in such a pursuit.

Paths to Prayer

Jesus and Mary
St. Mary's Hall, Villanova University, Villanova, Pennsylvania

Walking Where Jesus Walked

his imaginary walk with Jesus has opened my world more than I ever could have anticipated. I did not know, or perhaps did not remember, for example, that Calvary and Golgotha were one and the same, that Capernaum had become a second home to Jesus or even that Bethlehem was also David's birthplace.

It is not likely that I will ever walk those consecrated lands where Jesus walked. But it is sweet to recall that when I was enrolled in the Beginner's Department of the church where I spent the first two decades of my life, for every Sunday then and many years thereafter, our class would line up after our lesson, and our teacher would hand us our Sunday School paper. Considered old-fashioned these days, they contained pictures and stories of Jesus' time here on earth—I always relished taking them home. It must have been there that my sense of "where Jesus walked" was cultivated, just one more pearl for me to cherish. It is with some sadness that I wonder what ever became of them.

For my purpose here, I have studied maps, which seem to come in all sizes of discovery. These lands have continued to undergo constant change, and constant movement of peoples. Your Bible probably contains several maps, and you may find them a helpful tool in many of the little tours taken throughout this book.

In fact, your Bible is an indispensable help as we make our way through the New Testament. Space has allowed me a limited framework in which to share the Scriptures, and I hope you will help me by reading the surrounding text of selected passages!

Nazareth

In the sixth month the angel Gabriel was sent by God to a town in Galilee called Nazareth . . . (Luke 1:26).

In those days Jesus came from Nazareth of Galilee and was baptized by John in the Jordan (Mark 1:9).

Nazareth was, of course, Jesus, Mary, and Joseph's hometown. It was the town where Jesus lived for thirty of His brief thirty-three years. Here He received His religious training, learned to be a craftsman, and, many believe, as the oldest in His family, helped care for His siblings until the time of His service as God's divine Son began.

What was it like—Nazareth? What did Jesus see? How did the land around Him look? Some believe that only about five hundred people lived in the village of Nazareth at Jesus' time. Despite its small size and hilly terrain, it was a trade crossroad that boasted a cosmopolitan climate. Nazareth was scorned by Jews, since the Romans, to whom they were forced to pay taxes, were in charge there.

Nazareth experienced much despair: Crusaders, Muslims, and the Ottoman Turks all fought for and ruled through the centuries. The city, however, retained its image as a place of piety.

It was of Nazareth that Jesus declared, "Truly I tell you, no prophet is accepted in the prophet's hometown" (Luke 4:24). Rejected there, He left. There is no record that He ever returned.

Dear God,
In urging us to "love one another," You have
implicitly placed upon us the responsibility to know
one another. Rejuvenate our minds! Help us to think
of Jesus as a child, playing with wood shavings
from Joseph's woodshop floor, skipping alongside
His mother Mary to draw water from the well,
and even realizing as He grew that His destiny
was to be the renewing Spring of Purity from
which the world has drawn ever since. Amen.

Bethlehem

In the time of King Herod, after Jesus was born in Bethlehem of Judea, wise men from the East came to Jerusalem, asking, "Where is the child who has been born king of the Jews? For we have observed his star rising . . ." (Matt. 2:1–2).

*O*h! Little town of Bethlehem, how still we see thee lie. . . . How often we have sung this, surely one of our most compelling Christmas carols. Our hearts quicken, even as we envision the stillness. And yet we know that in that humble, quiet stable, a newly born baby was probably howling His little heart out! Jesus, so divine—Jesus, so human—had been born.

And what of Jesus' birthplace, the town called Bethlehem, so ripe with history? Dating back to approximately 1250 B.C., this ancient city is located about seven miles from Nazareth. Perched high above the hills, yet known for its fertile countryside, the word Bethlehem means "The House of Bread." Noting the symbolism takes no effort whatsoever! Jesus *is* the bread, the feast of our lives! Many scholars believe that Jesus, however, was not born in a traditional stable, but rather in a cave-stable, which was more characteristic of the way the villagers carved out their stables along the sloping hillside. Bethlehem was devastated in the second century by the Roman Emperor Hadrian, yet two centuries later, Helena, mother of Constantine, had "The Church of the Nativity" erected above the site believed to have been Jesus' birthplace-stable. It remains to this day a hallowed shrine.

Dear God,
We bow our heads in awe of the imagined moment of Jesus' birth. We cannot believe such magnificent love as Yours to have sent Your Son to us. How can we ever be worthy of such a gift? And yet we know that You accept us. We know it because You have revealed Yourself to us in so many wonderful ways. Witness the treasured moments we spend with friends and family, especially at Christmastime and special quiet moments reserved for friend-sharing alone. Carve into our lives a special place for Yourself this Christmas. Enter our hearts now and stay close by us as we anticipate the sanctity of Jesus' birth once again. Amen.

Sea of Galilee

As Jesus passed along the Sea of Galilee, he saw Simon and his brother Andrew casting a net into the sea—for they were fishermen. And Jesus said to them, "Follow me and I will make you fish for people." And immediately they left their nets and followed him (Mark 1:16–18).

This major event in Biblical history—Jesus appealing to men heretofore unknown to Him to follow Him—took place after Jesus had been baptized by John and His subsequent temptation by Satan. The Sea of Galilee was the site of many of the most exciting stories which fell on our innocent, childhood hearts: the calming of the storm; Jesus walking on water; the boy, his fish, and the feeding of the five thousand.

Around this heart-shaped sea in Palestine were several flourishing cities. They included Capernaum, Bethsaida, and, the only one now in existence, Tiberias. Nearly seven hundred feet below sea level, the River Jordan ran through it. The sea was laden with fish—nearly forty different kinds. Fruit and other kinds of agriculture grew there. Positioned between mountains, it was subject to violent winds and storms.

The region had a tropical climate and was known for its "warm sulphur springs." In order to take advantage of its therapeutic value, Herod built his palace near its waters. That may have been why so many sick came to the lakeshore appealing to Jesus. Or, could it have been that Jesus often walked along the shore because He not only drew from its serenity Himself, but He knew many were ill whom His love could heal?

Dear God,
How often we come to You for healing. Sometimes we
ask that You heal our bodies or that of someone we
love. Sometimes we need our hearts healed, or our
minds, and sometimes even our souls. In Your love,
which surrounds us like warm and healing water, we
know that we can immerse ourselves, finding renewal in
the purity of Your promise to us to make us Your own.
Help us to imagine You, real and alive, as You walked
along the shores of Galilee. Perhaps its waters even
gave You strength. Amen.

Galilee

Jesus went throughout Galilee, teaching in their synagogues and proclaiming the good news of the kingdom and curing every disease and every sickness among the people. So his fame spread throughout all Syria . . . (Matt. 4:23–24).

Jesus conducted his major ministry in Galilee. Why would Jesus have chosen this place? Dating back to almost 1500 B.C., Galilee is located in Northern Palestine. It was much like Nazareth: a caravan route, the site of many battles, and a cosmopolitan, commercially prominent place. Galileans were endowed with a certain sophistication, having been exposed to new ideas. Theirs was a mixed population, but most were Gentiles. Its many villages were thickly populated; fertile land made it even more appealing as a place to live. The land was tilled and tilled again; olives, oil, grains, and fish were exported.

All of these reasons help explain why Jesus may have taught here, but one more must be considered: Galileans, because of their wide experiences, were "bendable" and known to be open to change. Barclay commented that, in all of Palestine, Galilee was probably the only place new ideas could flourish. (Contemporarily, it is sad to note that its fertile lands have since turned to scrub and many of the places where Jesus walked have simply vanished.)

Here Jesus taught His Sermon on the Mount. Here He taught us the magic of storytelling and the seeds of Christian beliefs through His parables. How thankful we are for this place called Galilee!

Dear God.

There are so many ways that we can learn about Jesus. Walking where He walked is such a lovely way to do it. It is a way that we can try to visualize the things He saw, the nature of the people around Him, even the food that He might have eaten.

Would that we would consider prayerfully the choices we must make. Surely You have left behind the golden threads of how to weave our lives and make courageous choices after Your example. Continuously flush through us the courage to walk in Your ways, and to feel "at home" more there than anywhere. Amen.

Capernaum

*When he returned to Capernaum after some days, it was reported that he
was at home. So many gathered around that there was no longer room for
them, not even in front of the door; and he was speaking the word to them
(Mark 2:1–2).*

Capernaum's population was mostly Jewish. This was the
city that tax collectors, a Roman centurion—and three
who were to become Jesus' disciples—came to call home.
Jesus performed so many miracles here that the gospel of
Matthew refers to Capernaum as Jesus' "own city."

Here is where the Bible stories of our childhood come to
life. Remember Zacchaeus the tax collector? And the centurion who, despite his Roman background, asked Jesus to
heal his servant? It was from Capernaum that Jesus called
Andrew, Matthew, and he whom Jesus named as the Rock of
His church—Peter! And how about the story Mark tells
about the faith of the friends who climbed to the rooftop
and let their sick friend down so that Jesus could heal him?
Jesus performed miracle after miracle here. Still, this was the
city that Jesus prophesied would meet with certain devasta-
tion (Matt. 11:23) because they refused to believe His
divine destiny.

The synagogue, which existed there for centuries, has
been undergoing extensive excavation, particularly since the
site was purchased by the Franciscan friars in 1894.
Excavations have revealed a distinctive white limestone
building of great size, "elaborately decorated with sculp-
tured representations of animals, plants," etc. Astoundingly,
it is believed to have been the very synagogue in which
Jesus preached!

Dear God,
Thank You for welcoming each of us into Your household. We know when we study Your world, that the very place in which You lived was neither private nor forbidden, even to strangers. In this You have shown us a wonderful Christian ethic—to welcome all, not only into our homes, but into our hearts. Amen.

Jerusalem

When he entered Jerusalem, the whole city was in turmoil, asking, "Who is this?" The crowds were saying, "This is the prophet Jesus from Nazareth in Galilee" (Matt. 21:10–11).

We arrive in Jerusalem with Jesus, and we learn that it was "in turmoil." It seems to have seldom been otherwise. Jesus brought little tranquility, for He went into the temple and "drove out all who were selling and buying in the temple . . ." Quickly changing this chaos into charity, Jesus began to heal the blind and lame before He traveled to Bethany.

Its heightened interest for us is that primarily it is steeped in the history of three of the world's major religions: to the Jews, it was the "city which the Lord had chosen out of all the tribes of Israel." It also became, around the seventh century, the place where Muslims believe that Mohammed ascended into heaven. The Russian Orthodox Church of Mary Magdalene was also built there. But for Christians, how could the place where Jesus was crucified, buried, and rose from the dead be anything less than sacred? This is the city that Jesus wept over, and where He lived the last week of His life. When we think of the Upper Room, His trial, and the crowds chanting for His persecution . . . this was Jerusalem!

Dear God,
In each of our imaginations, we treasure a glimpse of
Jesus' entry into Jerusalem, riding astride a donkey,
and of the events which quickly evolved thereafter,
seemingly without a pause, until Jesus' flimsy trial
and final triumph and sacrifice. These are precious
thoughts, sacred to each of us. As Christians, we know
what they mean to our individual pilgrimages here on
earth. As such, they can only become more invaluable
with each passing day of our lives, making our
passage here all the more satisfying. Amen.

Golgotha (Calvary)

So they took Jesus; and carrying the cross by himself, he went out to what is called The Place of the Skull, which in Hebrew is called Golgotha (John 19:16–17).

*A*lso known as Calvary, the precise site of Jesus' crucifixion has not yet been agreed upon by even the most ardent scholars. (Jerusalem was destroyed in A.D. 70; in rebuilding it, the exact location was obliterated.) We do know that it was close to Jerusalem and near the side of a busy road, and probably on a hilly place, where such common executions could be visible for a distance. Exposing such gruesome punishment was believed to be a visible deterrent to crime. Since the fourth century, the Church of the Holy Sepulcher "has been revered" as the location of Calvary.

Whichever road Jesus took after his trial, several incidents occurred. We know them as the Twelve Stations of the Cross. They begin with Pilate's condemnation of Jesus and end with Jesus being laid to rest in the sepulcher.

As familiar as the name Calvary is to us (remember that old favorite hymn, *Lead Me to Calvary?*), it is only mentioned once in the Bible—in the gospel of Luke.

Dear God,
Our hearts tremble when we remember the sight of
You on the cross. Our minds marvel at its mystery.
And yet we know that it is the only way—entering
through the cross—that we can ever expect to make
the journey into the kind of perfected Christianhood
which takes us into the foreverafter.

How can we ever thank You for Your selfless life,
and all that it taught us? Amen.

Rose Window
Bryn Mawr Presbyterian Church, Bryn Mawr, Pennsylvania

Jesus Chooses His Disciples

Beyond a few facts, I have always thought collectively about the disciples. These portraits are an attempt to single them out and highlight their various characteristics and contributions as Jesus' chosen stewards. They asked the questions we might have asked if we had the courage. As in any study, there are always inconsistencies, but they have been tackled as knowledgeably as possible. On a personal note, I have tried to place the disciples in their historic times, and yet portray them, however briefly, as infinitely human beings.

Jesus chose His disciples from several vocations. We know, of course, of the fishermen, Peter and Andrew among them, and of the unlikely tax collector-turned-disciple, Matthew. In several cases, we not only do not know their profession, we know very little in any context. Many did not seem extraordinary, but we are among those made whole through the centuries by virtue of their early devotion.

There were three sets of brothers, perhaps to remind us that siblings really can get along well together, especially when they focus on the good, the true, and the beautiful.

Philip–The Spontaneous Skeptic

The next day Jesus decided to go to Galilee. He found Philip and said to him, "Follow me." Philip found Nathanael and said to him, "We have found him about whom Moses in the law and also the prophets wrote, Jesus son of Joseph from Nazareth" (John 1:43, 45).

Philip said to him, "Lord, show us the Father, and we will be satisfied." Jesus said to him, "Have I been with you all this time, Philip, and you still do not know me?" (John 14:8–9).

Among the first to be called, we learn something of Jesus' decision-making process in the way that He so assuredly called Philip. One wonders what Jesus observed in Philip to have given him this sudden place of distinction.

Philip was tested by Jesus when He asked how the disciples could ever feed such a crowd assembled on the mountain. "Six months' wages would not buy enough bread for each of them to get a little," the skeptical Philip responded. And it was Philip who prompted Jesus' long response quoted briefly above, and which we should refresh ourselves by rereading. Philip, so excitedly sure in the first case, is found questioning Jesus, not once, but twice! His faithfulness, however, cannot be questioned, for he was at Jesus' side when he was crucified and, there again in the upper room after Jesus' ascension.

Dear God,
Spontaneity requires we not question our hearts
before we begin to question our minds. Philip
encountered Jesus with an open heart.
Beginning this very moment, we can experience
lovely encounters with Christ every day of our lives,
if we seek Him with a loving and open heart. Amen.

Peter and Andrew—
The Bond of Brothers

As Jesus passed along the Sea of Galilee, he saw Simon and his brother Andrew casting a net into the sea—for they were fishermen. And Jesus said to them, "Follow me and I will make you fish for people." And immediately they left their nets and followed him (Mark 1:16–18).

Both Andrew and Simon Peter had been followers of John the Baptist. From the moment they met Jesus, however, neither hesitated to leave the known behind. In Andrew, Jesus must have recognized faithful and quiet characteristics; in Peter, He must have recognized a man of such dynamism that He immediately changed his name to Cephas (Peter), meaning "rock."

Jesus visited their home where their family's hospitality was well known. Jesus cured Peter's mother-in-law there and, later that day, "the whole city" gathered around while Jesus continued to perform His miracles. It is comforting to think of them as friends.

In contrast to Philip, Andrew assuaged Jesus' concern for the five thousand by volunteering that there was a boy with five loaves and two fishes. Not among Jesus' inner circle, and despite Peter's prominence, Andrew remained with Jesus.

Always topping the list of the disciples, we know more about Peter than any other disciple. Spokesman for the Twelve, it was Peter who responded to Christ's question, "But who do you say that I am?" with the unequivocal, "You are the Messiah." Alas! We do remember his denial, even as we fail to remember that while other disciples fled in those treacherous moments of Jesus' capture, he remained. Peter is believed to have been martyred in Rome.

Dear God,
From Andrew, we learn that respect and love
can dissolve rivalry, for he allowed Peter
the limelight. Peter's leadership, nearly overshadowed
by his unquestionable act of disloyalty, reminds us of
our humanness and Jesus' forgiveness. We may
tremble, but not fall. Amen.

James and John—"Sons of Thunder"

This is the disciple who is testifying to these things and has written them, and we know that his testimony is true. But there are also many other things that Jesus did; if every one of them were written down, I suppose that the world itself could not contain the books that would be written (John 21:24–25).

James and John, sons of Zebedee, appear among the top four in every listing of Jesus' disciples. Both were present with Jesus at Gethsamane, along with Peter. In Acts we learn that James later became the first Christian martyr. John's identity has been conjectured—not proven—to be that of Jesus' "Beloved Disciple," and perhaps the mysterious author of the fourth gospel. Both were fishermen. Known for their brash temperaments, we have no question that their mother would ask Jesus if her sons could sit by Him in Glory.

Scholars find fertile ground for disagreement on the question of whether this John was the author of the fourth gospel. I favor the inspired theory that the John who authored the fourth gospel was the Beloved Disciple, whom Jesus' grace transformed from contentious to convert.

Here I offer a compass to a book of majesty. The gospel of John does not begin with Jesus' birth, but with the beginning. There are no parables; there are "signs." Passages use symbolic opposites like "light" and "dark." Its poetic and mysterious narrative is the only gospel which unravels Jesus' ministry over three years. Whoever the Beloved Disciple was, we cannot question his status before Jesus, since he "reclined" next to Jesus at the Last Supper, and he was the one Jesus asked to care for His mother at the resurrection. You can never quite be the same after reading John!

Dear God,
James and John's faithfulness is astonishing.
They were so much of what we can be—
angry and ambitious. Then, after knowing
Jesus—faithful, inspired, and loving.
Such gifts are ours forevermore and all we
ever need to feel Thy peace and grace. Amen.

Matthew (Levi) and James, Sons of Alphaeus

After this he went out and saw a tax collector named Levi, sitting at the tax booth; and he said to him, "Follow me." And he got up, left everything, and followed him (Luke 5:27).

Imagine! Imagine how magnetic a personality Jesus was to anyone who opened themselves to Him, even this tax collector who was despised by all! And yet we learn that he "left everything" and followed Jesus. Luke continues his story, telling us that Matthew invited Jesus to a feast in his home. Jesus accepted, receiving scorn Himself in the process. Jesus' response is well known: "I have come to call not the righteous but sinners to repentance."

From the phrase "left everything," we can deduce that Luke is telling us that Matthew was quite wealthy, since his position as a tax collector meant that he collected taxes not only from local merchants, but also from caravans passing through Capernaum, the city where Matthew lived.

Again, the author of the gospel of Matthew is disputed, but William Barclay declares that, "ancient tradition is unanimous" that Matthew wrote a gospel in Hebrew. Whoever its author, we are grateful, for we find an easy-to-read narrative, which includes the Beatitudes, many miracles, and Jesus' clear directive: "Go ye therefore and teach all nations." Matthew leans heavily on Old Testament prophecies, convincing us that Matthew was a Jew-turned-Christian.

We know little of James, except agreement that he was Matthew's brother. This is our third set of brother-disciples. Surely Jesus meant for Christianity to be a family affair.

Dear God,
Help us to truly use the gifts You've given us.
Open our eyes to the different kinds of
helpers we can be. May we use our gifts wisely,
insofar as we are able. Amen.

Questioning Nathanael and/or Bartholomew

When Jesus saw Nathanael coming toward him, he said of him, "Here is truly an Israelite in whom there is no deceit!" Nathanael asked him, "Where did you get to know me?" Jesus answered, "I saw you under the fig tree. . . ." Nathanael replied, "Rabbi, you are the Son of God!" (John 1:47–49).

Most scholars believe that Nathanael and/or Bartholomew are actually the same person, but are reluctant to rule out the possibility that they may, in fact, be two separate people.

The New Testament tells us nothing whatsoever about Bartholomew, although he is mentioned in the first three gospels, Nathanael only in John. However, we cannot quibble about the fact that Nathanael knew and spoke with Jesus, since John has recorded this familiar biblical conversation.

It was Nathanael who asked, "Can anything good come out of Nazareth?" Some scholars interpret this as brash; others are convinced that because Nathanael was a rigid scholar—maybe even a mystic—Nathanael could hardly believe *in the most profound sense* Philip's announcement that he had found the Messiah. Jesus gives us the clue that Nathanael was a scholar, for Jesus had seen Nathanael under the fig tree, a sheltering, quiet place just outside one's home where those who wished to pray and study would go. John tells us that Nathanael was among those faithful gathered by the Sea of Galilee after the resurrection. How wonderful to be remembered as having "no deceit!"

Dear God,
Stories of people like Nathanael ripen our faith
even more, making it all the easier for us to share
our faith, not our doubts. Christians are at home
with mysteries! How grateful we are that we are
beyond the need to see in order to believe. Amen.

Despairing Judas Iscariot

When Judas, his betrayer, saw that Jesus was condemned, he repented and brought back the thirty pieces of silver. . . . But they said, "What is that to us?" . . . and he went and hanged himself (Matt. 27:3–5).

"I guarded them, and not one of them was lost except the one destined to be lost. . . ." (John 17–12).

Nothing is known about the manner in which Jesus chose Judas, but we know that he held the trusted position of treasurer of the Twelve. His name, sadly, has become a synonym for evil.

Judas' encounters with Jesus sowed the seeds of doubt about his character. Remember he chided Jesus for allowing Mary of Bethany to waste precious oil to anoint Jesus' feet? Some scholars are convinced Judas believed Jesus to be the long-anticipated, earthly king. As treasurer, the royal purse would be accessible to him. This could explain why he did not want Jesus "to be delivered" to authorities who would kill him. Others maintain that he believed if he forced Jesus' hand, Jesus could save Himself under any circumstances. Hardly unaware of Judas' nature, those are Jesus' words speaking about the "one destined to be lost."

Scholars have speculated endlessly on how anyone could have been so close to Jesus and been responsible for such an anguishing lapse of character. The fact remains that no matter how we try, we cannot understand such dark motives. Perhaps all we need to understand is that Judas sold his heart, and that we, as much as we in all our humanness wish not to think of it, have often experienced the frail fear of failing, or falling, far below the purest of Christian standards.

Dear God,
Judas' story teaches us of the misery we face when
we wander into the dangerous reaches of our own
misguided desires. Repent, we can; but often retracing
our steps does not offer pure consolation. May
we ever be mindful of how our actions can
adversely affect others as well. Amen.

Thomas, Judas, and Simon the Zealot—
Doubter, Activist, and Nationalist

Thomas said to him,"Lord, we do not know where you are going. How can we know the way?" (John 14:5).

Thomas

*T*hese words, spoken at the Last Supper, contain a question we ourselves have asked. Thomas posed this question in one of the Bible's most familiar and comforting segments which begins: "Do not let your hearts be troubled. . . ." and continues after Thomas' question with, "I am the way, and the truth, and the life." Thomas exhibited further doubt when he asked to see Jesus' hands and side after the resurrection. A true seeker of truth, perhaps we should admit that his disbelief helps to cure our own!

Judas

Judas (not Iscariot) said to him, "Lord, how is it that you are revealing yourself to us and not the world?" (John 14:18).

We know very little about this Judas, except that he was a political activist who could not understand why, if Jesus was revealing His true identity, He would not exploit it. Surely Jesus could change the world! Jesus' response was that love was the foundation of His mission, that putting love into action was the kind of activism which would most closely portray Jesus' real authority. Activists are often impatient, but their questions can make us think!

Simon the Zealot

We know nothing whatsoever about Simon, except that he was a Zealot, variously defined as a member of a "radical political party working for the overthrow of Roman rule in Israel," or the softened designation of "enthusiast for God." However we wish to define it, either of these meanings leave no uncertainty that Simon lived his life in anything but neutral. Once again, we are confronted with the ineffable presence of Jesus to accept—and attract—such a man.

Dear God,
We prize our individualism, but we pray that
You will keep us strong enough to understand
our weaknesses in a way that allows You to calm
and guide our souls always. Amen.

Jesus' Baptism
Grace Episcopal Church, Topeka, Kansas

The Good Shepherd
Gethsemane Cemetery, Detroit, Michigan

Blessed Are the Pure in Heart
Southwestern Presbyterian Church, Philadelphia, Pennsylvania

Plain Talk about the Beatitudes

In Matthew 5:1 we read what I consider to be a verse which sets with great and simple clarity a mood and quality about Jesus' true nature. For a moment, let our minds wander. Let us visualize Jesus sitting down and seizing the moment when His new disciples and crowds gathered around Him "on a hillside near Capernaum"—grand teacher that He was—to share with these people a way of approaching and living their lives in anything but a vague or tepid fashion. The verse reads: "When Jesus saw the crowds, he went up the mountain; and after he sat down his disciples came to him. Then he began to speak, and taught them, saying . . ."

Thus begins a series of eight sayings which read, learned, and spoken by us (often as children) we have handed down to those we love. Each begins with the word "blessed," which in Greek (*makarios*) is translated as "happy." This repetitive approach was not unusual in those times, but rather helped to concretize the path to ethics, morality, and an indefinable serenity. Someone once wrote that the Beatitudes recognize that the "higher righteousness is not attained by a larger total of good deeds, but it is the fruit of a life transformed by the grace of God."

Many sources emphasize the fact that the Beatitudes were not set down in one sermon given by Jesus. Rather, they are the "essence of all that Jesus continuously and habitually" taught His disciples. Each beatitude is to be savored incrementally; expect some mystery to remain. Summed up, where else could one find such a concise recipe for ways of resolving the varied conflicts of life?

Those Poor in Spirit

Blessed are the poor in spirit for theirs is the kingdom of heaven (Matt. 5:3).

Scholars generally agree that probably the most powerful idea set forth in the New Testament is that of the "kingdom of heaven," as the gospel of Matthew puts it, or "Kingdom of God," the phrase used by Mark and Luke. I think each of us has read and prayed enough that our hearts understand and are comfortable with its spiritual implications in our own lives. It is within this personal and prayerful context that we can most contentedly come to the hillside with Jesus and listen to His words.

Certainly this beatitude speaks to those among us who are "economically deprived." But we must also consider that this beatitude beckons those willing to "stand before God with no illusions of self-righteousness or self-sufficiency." We all know how far from God someone seems when they are lost in their own self-righteousness. How can God be with us when we are insisting that there is none other than our own perfect way? This beatitude invites us to strip away our pride and allow ourselves to be immersed in God's loving care forevermore.

Have you ever noticed how exhausting it can be to be in the company of someone who is self-righteous? Perhaps we even recognize these traits in ourselves!

Dear God,
This is a first step most of us have to take again
and again in life. We seem to need to constantly
remind ourselves that neither we nor anyone
around us can satisfy our most basic needs, let
alone our innermost longings. Only those who
can acknowledge how "poor in spirit" we are
can ever reach that "ineffably sublime"
state that makes us sing.

Make us children of trust, as we put our hand in
Yours and walk close by Your side, as we
make our way through the low—as well as the
high—tide waters of life. Amen.

Those Who Mourn

Blessed are those who mourn, for they shall be comforted (Matt. 5:4).

We cannot know the hearts which this beatitude has helped heal. There is no mystery here; only the assurance that our broken heart will be comforted, especially after the loss of someone we love, when we place ourselves in God's loving care. This is healing in one of its purest forms.

Mourning wears many different faces, however. My dictionary offers several definitions: "a deep distress, sadness, or regret. . . ." I have mourned because something I have said has been hurtful; I have mourned over pieces of sadness which have come marching into my children's lives; I have mourned for the family, unknown to me except by virtue of television, who lost a member to the excesses of war. I have mourned because people seem to shout without listening, and to take without asking. I have mourned for the loss of a soul who cannot seem to stay in the grip of God's steadfast love, no matter how compassionately we try to make our case. And so have you.

Dear God,
Comfort us as only You can as we wrestle with
our often imperceptible lifetime losses. Help us to
remember with joy the happiness we experienced
with the great loves of our lives whom we have lost,
and to thank You for the gift of such penetrating
love that arouses in us such passionate mourning.

On other occasions, when we know how shattering
life can be as it is experienced for others whom we
will never know, except as our earthly brothers
and sisters, help us to know that even awareness
of their suffering may in some way become the
beginning of the cure of caring. Amen.

Those Who Are Meek

Blessed are the meek, for they shall inherit the earth (Matt. 5:5).

Again I turn to the dictionary, for Jesus is using a word little heard in our contemporary society. Does this beatitude have relevance today? It reads: "enduring injury with patience and without resentment. . . ." Another dictionary states: "humbly patient, forbearing, gentle. . . ."

Now we experience some difficulty. Do I know of someone actually capable of perhaps not entirely over-looking, but looking beyond, one's own pain and accepting—in effect, "Thy will be done?" We all do, for we all have our everyday angels and heroes. Helen Keller is an example of this in action, as she was ultimately able to dissolve the demons within her and live a life which was beckoning, not beaten. Franklin D. Roosevelt was a man of real derring-do who insisted that his entire life not become unalterably interrupted because of the onset of infantile paralysis.

All injuries are not physical, of course. Mental or emotional stress are crippling in their own way. Perhaps what we are looking for here is enough wisdom to understand that life does sometimes veer beyond our control, and sometimes very critically. We then need to bring ourselves back into some kind of balance, and acknowledge that we do have the power to live our lives without the acid of bitterness which can spill over onto others we care about, overriding anything we could have ever hoped to accomplish.

Dear God,
When life's wear and tear show signs of threatening
to overwhelm us, when feeling sorry for ourselves
becomes our way of life, reinforce our will not
to be thrown off balance. Our actions personally
affect those dear to us. Thinking of others may be
just the antidote we need to regain our own sense of
composure in a way that helps us to react to the
unexpected in a confident and prayerful way. Amen.

Those Who Hunger After Righteousness

Blessed are those who hunger and thirst for righteousness, for they will be filled (Matt. 5:6).

$\mathcal{N}$ ot one of us is unaware of the hunger that exists in every corner of this earth. And there are probably few of us who have not tried to alleviate this inhuman kind of pain. May we coax ourselves to expand this particular mission in our lives in as many ways as we are able.

If there remains a certain mystery in some of the Beatitudes, certainly there is little mystery in this one, in both its literal and figurative meanings. This beatitude begs the question: How willing are we to give up the things of this world in order to move closer to the serene principles Jesus so long ago taught? If we stumble over an old-fashioned word here and there, if we cannot seem to find the precise meaning of a phrase, or if we wish to argue with precepts that we think we understand but find difficult to accept, may we realize that this process of discovery draws us ever closer to the lives we should be living.

We are, curiously, moving away from the enticements of this world, and living lives closer to God's holy realm *without even realizing it!*

Dear God,
May we indeed hunger after righteousness as if our
human existence depended upon it for
a source of nourishment without which we simply
could not live. Help us not to think we have been
"good," help us just to be good. In trying to keep
a sense of balance, may we finally come to a
cherished place where goodness-thinking is as
balanced and natural as rain and a source of
energy in and of itself. Amen.

Those Who Are Merciful

Blessed are the merciful, for they will receive mercy (Matt. 5:7).

The word "mercy" in Hebrew means to actually exchange places with someone, and to make a deliberate effort to understand another's source of pain—certainly more easily said than done!

People who live merciful lives are truly revered. They seem to have come by the stepping stones of grace inherently. We have learned to identify their characteristics: they are anything but self-absorbed; they ask, "How are you?" and mean it! They become absolute necessities in the lives of their friends and family. And I am fortunate enough to know true models.

Of the merciful, the selfless, the kindly image of Mother Teresa streams into one's mind. Of Albanian heritage, from the age of twelve she sensed a calling to let her life be lived through Christ or, in her words, "to serve him among the poorest of the poor." Eventually, she established an order which became known as The Missionaries of Charity, an order presently of such magnitude that it ministers to the poor worldwide. While her life's work was carried out chiefly in India, when she died in 1997, few could deny that she belonged to the world, yet cared little for the esteem it poured upon her. *Blessed are the merciful.*

Dear God,
Help us to avoid the temptation of
becoming part of this "me first" society
in which we live. Help us to find within ourselves
the desire to wear another's shoes whenever we are able.
Give us the energy and interest that we need to do it
more often than we might either be inclined or think
ourselves capable. May we find loving opportunities
to open our hearts to someone else's heartache.
We ask You to help us find the appropriate
balance between overstretching ourselves until we
find, in fact, that we may need mercy extended
to us and, thereby, drain a source which may
be taken away from someone else's need. Amen.

The Pure In Heart

Blessed are the pure in heart, for they shall see God (Matt. 5:8).

In Greek, "pure" has several meanings, but all rolled up into one, it means "unmixed, unadulterated"—like pure gold. In this most ingratiating of the Beatitudes, Jesus is imploring us to lead a life of unmasked motives.

Ursula King's book, *Christian Mystics*, is a book of magical illumination. I did not grow up in a tradition in which saints were part of our Christian education, however familiar some names were. King's perception is that mystics "offer a message of wholeness and healing, of harmony, peace, and joy; also of immense struggles fought and won." Tenth-century German mystic, musician, painter, and poet Hildegard of Bingen was "dedicated to the church at birth." A recent revival of her music has been defined as "unpretentious and thrilling. . . ." Her purity comes down to us—a gift of the ages.

Of course, life has never been free of competitiveness, contentiousness, or me-firstness, and these characteristics are particularly not easy to shrug off in our time. Can we live a life free of such saddling? This beatitude forces us, as difficult as it is, to search our own souls and ask why we do certain, questionable things. In our time, it may even mean elimination of the "it would look good on my resume" mentality. Self-examination is not very easy, but occasional check-ups have been known to work wonders!

Dear God,
Help us to keep our thoughts and motives
unmasked. May we be more concerned about our
own actions than we give others cause to be. In a
world where it is impossible to make our way
without the help, interest, and love of others, help us
not to use those with whom we are associated and,
perhaps, love, in some untoward way to make
some perceived progress for ourselves. Keep us on the
honest course. We can only accomplish this if we
search our own souls and seek out what it is that
You would have us do—and then do it. Amen.

Those Who Are Peacemakers

Blessed are the peacemakers, for they shall be called the children of God (Matt. 5:9).

Shalom, the Hebrew word for "peace," means not only "the absence of evil things," but the wish for "the presence of all good things." Peacemaking, if we yield to the opportunities which come our way to be a peacemaker, can bring sublime pleasure, even though we may be "rocking the boat."

We can hardly bring the dignity he deserves into our limited space here, but Dag Hammarskjold, who was the second secretary-general of the United Nations, originated the idea of UN emergency forces to help mediate problems between belligerent countries. "A devout but private Christian," he lived for the cause of international peace until his death in an unexplained airplane accident while on a peace mission to Africa. His name is indispensably tied to the heart of peacemaking and peacekeeping. Perhaps some of you have seen Marc Chagall's stained glass memorial to Dag Hammarskjold "associated with the theme of peace" at the United Nations headquarters in New York City.

Being a peacemaker seldom requires us to risk our lives; but it might require inserting ourselves into a children's playtime gone awry, occasionally abandoning our "let them settle it themselves" attitude. It may also mean encouraging conversations which have drifted into denigrating another's character to move down another lane. Passivity, at times, can only cause more trouble. This beatitude challenges us to be among those of God's children who attempt to bring understanding in an effort to smooth the bumpy passages of life.

Dear God,
Help us to be counted among those who light the
candles of helpfulness and not snuff them out.
Help us to heal the wounds that words
and actions can inflict, especially between and
among those we love. May we learn how to
gracefully bury hurt and not dredge it up to justify
continued bitterness in any of its ugly forms.
May nothing blight our intense desire to dedicate
ourselves to being a child of God. Amen.

Blessed Are Those Who Are Persecuted

Blessed are those who are persecuted for righteousness' sake, for theirs is the kingdom of heaven. Blessed are you when people revile you and persecute you and utter all kinds of evil against you falsely on my account (Matt. 5:10–11).

The reforming ideas that German theologian Dietrich Bonhoeffer advanced in the cause of a "unitive" world church were far before their time. Bonhoeffer could not tolerate the sweeping arc of Hitler's tyranny. For his "marginal" involvement in the conspiracy against Hitler's life, Bonhoeffer was executed in 1945 at the age of thirty-nine.

I have had the gift of irrepressibly lovely friendships in my life, cultivated over many years. One of them was the mother of my Armenian friend, Florence. I was privileged to know and love her mother, who was ninety-four when she died. I often sat enchanted at Florence's kitchen table, chatting with Mrs. Proodian about her growing up years. Armenian history is burdened with conquest, persecution, starvation, and even "attempted extermination." Devoted to both her homeland and her church, Mrs. Proodian grew up in Smyrna, which became part of Turkey in the early 1920s and is now known as Izmir. There was a kind of sorrow about her, and yet it never overtook all the beautiful things she was. I came to believe that grace was her constant companion, passed naturally down through successive generations.

Following Christian paths has never been easy; but neither can we ever say that Jesus ever misled us into thinking it would be! We need only to consider His own sacrificial life.

Dear God,
Without being presumptuous, we know that
sometimes we are the conscience of others.
This is a serious condition.
We know that such times put us
at risk with society, and
sometimes even with our friends and family.
Help us to accept such a course,
if need be, and to realize that such an unavoidable
struggle brings us one step closer
to the reality of Your eternal presence. Amen.

Sermon on the Mount
First Baptist Church, Augusta, Georgia

Plain Talk about the Parables

Biblical scholars find rich clay with which to mold their theories about the meaning, purpose, and significance of the New Testament parables. The word itself is even variously defined in Greek as "riddle," or even "a comparison."

St. Augustine, for example, assigned every character and action in the parable of the Good Samaritan a symbol representing some tenet of Christian faith. Later scholars argue that a parable loses its "effectiveness" when one tries to attach "meaning to every detail." Even the number of New Testament parables is contested: Perhaps there are sixty, but some say as few as thirty.

The Kingdom of God, a phrase conjuring up the purest of images, is regarded as the most galvanizing New Testament concept, but also the most problematic. Still tingling in my mind is the definition one of our pastors offered in a sermon on the Kingdom of God. He said something like this: Scholars may argue about its meaning, but I prefer to think that this church and the people who come here, and what they try to do are much like what we can expect the Kingdom of God to be.

For most of us, however, these stories do not have to be fine tooth-combed to give us comfort. In them we found— perhaps long ago—that cradled in our hearts, they were simplified enough to point out some magnificent truths capable of having instantaneous and life-long impact. Jesus accomplished this, Master teacher that He was, by avoiding the abstract and instead interesting his audience with familiar threads of their lives.

Memorized by many of us when we were children, the parables still tantalize the grown-up heart and mind and coax one further down the path Jesus Himself would have us go.

The Parable of the Weeds (Thistles)

"The kingdom of heaven may be compared to someone who sowed good seed in his field; but while everybody was asleep, an enemy came and sowed weeds among the wheat . . ." (Matt. 13:24–25).

Then he left the crowds and went into the house. And his disciples approached him, saying, "Explain to us the parable of the weeds. . . ." He answered, "The one who sows the good seed is the Son of Man; the field is the world, and the good seed are the children of the kingdom; the weeds are the children of the evil one, and the enemy who sowed them is the devil . . ." (Matt. 13:36–39).

In the first of these compelling passages, Jesus compares the good seed with the bad— a parable that would seem, on the face of it, simple enough to understand. Jesus then goes on to tell the parables of the mustard seed and the yeast.

But it is the parable of the thistles which attracts the disciples' interest; later they ask Jesus to explain it. My Bible offers this explanation: the young thistles so closely resembled the young blades of wheat that it was impossible to tell them apart. They also had a propensity to become tangled, one with the other, and could not be "distinguished" until they were grown. This meant that, during the growing period, they thrived side-by-side. Jesus is telling us that in our earthly lives, we "grow together until the harvest," then the weeds will be burned, but the wheat gathered. What then awaits us, according to this parable, is nothing less than the Kingdom of Heaven.

Dear God,
We find that we, too, often have difficulty sorting
out both the good and the bad grains of our lives.
Sometimes we don't even want to. Often when we
find ourselves caught in the midst of tangles, we
look around for someone else to blame, not
wanting to see before us our own image.
Help us to defeat these mischievous spirits
which come to play in our souls.

We know that You understand the fragility of
our human nature. Lead us away from the folly
of blaming our shortcomings on others;
help us instead to be reflectors of our faith. Amen.

The Parable of the Mustard Seed

He also said, "With what can we compare the kingdom of God, or what parable will we use for it? It is like a mustard seed, which, when sown upon the ground, is the smallest of all the seeds on earth; yet when it is sown it grows up and becomes the greatest of all shrubs, and puts forth large branches, so that the birds of the air can make nests in its shade" (Mark 4:30).

Sometimes growing twelve feet tall, the mustard plant grew along the "fertile plains of Gennesaret," a place where Jesus often encountered the crowds following Him. Commonly grown around Palestine, it had multiple uses—oil, condiments, and even as an herb. Since this parable appears in the first three gospels, we can comfortably infer that Jesus was using a popular expression of the times, and making a point He did not want overlooked. Jesus chose the tiny mustard seed to remind us that even if our faith begins as the size of a mustard seed, "nothing would be impossible."

If we make believe that we are among the crowds hungry to hear Jesus, we can see that His parables fit like pieces into a heavenly whole. For Jesus had started with one disciple, then two, until he had the Twelve. Their purpose was certainly unclear to them in the beginning, but Jesus nurtured them along, until this disparate group of men built the seeds of what was to become Christ's worldwide church.

Dear God,
Remembering that the tiniest of seeds can become
the most bountiful of plants, let us abandon our
own speculation and give in to the inspirations of
our hearts. Help us to realize that no matter how
small our beginning, it is the most important step
we can take. We can make a difference; we can be
forces for good. You always keep us in touch with
those thoughts if we allow You to do so.
Remind us that moving that imaginary mountain
we fear just a mite may lighten someone's heart
and our own as well.

Help us not be to afraid—or reluctant—to begin
seemingly hard things. Amen.

The Parable of the Growing Wheat

"The kingdom of God is as if someone would scatter seed on the ground, and would sleep and rise night and day, and the seed would sprout and grow, he does not know how. But when the grain is ripe, at once he goes in with his sickle, because the harvest has come" (Mark 4:26–27, 29).

Who can truly explain how a seed grows? What we can express is how visceral we feel when we experience success, particularly with some hard-go-grow plant. We often learn about this kind of success as a child, when equipped with all we need—a paper cup, some soil, and a seed—we watch the magic of growth occur right before our eyes. This often requires abundant patience.

I have a "Daniel" story. Daniel is one of my grandchildren. Sparks of curiosity can often be detected across his dear face. Now five, when he was three, he asked his mother what would happen if he planted a lemon seed. When it was a few inches high, it became my Christmas present a couple of years ago. My sprouting lemon tree is now nearly two feet high, and sports the shiniest green leaves. But, as you can see, that lemon tree did not grow overnight. Slow growing, patience—and interest—were required! Watching God at work, Daniel often checks out his lemon tree!

Dear God,
How anxious we allow ourselves to become.
We hurry through the days despite their complexion—
good days where we encounter joy and bad
days when we encounter despair. Help us to be
more even-handed with the moments of our lives and
treat them with more respect and enthusiasm.

Our spiritual growth often encounters the same
shock waves of up-and-downness. Teach us
patience that will stretch our spirituality evenly over
the expansiveness of our lives. Torn spirituality causes
such unnecessary suffering. If we can learn to
understand our own nature and treat it respectfully,
then we can expect to find an ever more highly
developed sense of Your own presence in our lives. Amen.

The Parable of the Precious Pearl

"Again, the Kingdom of Heaven is like a merchant in search of fine pearls; on finding one pearl of great value, he went and sold all that he had and bought it" (Matt. 13:45–46).

$\mathcal{I}$n the ancient world pearls were zealously sought after and treasured, even as they are today. In Revelation we glean the importance of pearls when we read, "the twelve gates of the new Jerusalem are described as twelve individual pearls." Found mostly around the Red Sea, they were treasured not only for their monetary value, but even more for their aesthetic beauty. Aware of this, we understand that the merchant who scoured the world markets, ultimately finding that one very remarkable pearl, experienced great joy, which was so complete that he sold all that belonged to him in order to possess this particular pearl—perhaps a gift for his bride!

The pearl in the parable, of course, is the Kingdom of God. We, if we are wise, are the merchant. When we think of God's Kingdom as the most sacred of pearls, we quickly understand that we can possess the God-given gifts of peace and harmony in our lives. Like this merchant, we have other good things in our lives, but in our hearts we know we possess the most lovely of all possessions when we feel at home in our heart's own Kingdom of God.

Dear God,

Sometimes we finally come to You as the result of some sudden burst of understanding. Others of us have come only after an arduous and complicated search. Whatever has been our road, we know that the pearls in Your Kingdom continue to dazzle us the farther along the road we travel and the deeper we search.

When we pray the prayer that challenges us to hold fast to that which is good, may it be the perfect pearl we know as Your Kingdom that we remember. Amen.

The Parable of the Fig Tree

A man had a fig tree planted in his vineyard; and he came looking for fruit on it and found none. So he said to the gardener, "See here! For three years I have come looking for fruit on this fig tree, and still I find none. Cut it down! Why should it be wasting the soil?" He replied, "Sir, let it alone for one more year. . . . If it bears fruit, well and good; but if not, you can cut it down" (Luke 13:6–9).

Again and again Jesus tempts us to goodness using the harvest of that richly cultivatable land around Palestine. The all-important fig tree was a natural topic for one of Jesus' parables, this being just one of several references to it. For all of the luscious fruit it *could* yield, it did require specific care. Fig trees were usually not cultivated in groves, but individually. Its large leaves gave wonderful shade; height and longevity made them an enviable tree close by small dwellings. Figs could make a plateful of colors, from purples to white, depending on the time of year they were harvested. Their productivity, however, depended on the absolute of patience.

In speaking of the unproductive nature of the fig tree, Jesus seems to be signaling that He knows we individuals require more than our share of patience to be productive. And with a bit of reflection, we understand that even God gets restless with our inattention and excuses to Him. Although the little fig tree was given a second chance, this parable tells us in no uncertain terms that uselessness—and taking but never giving—invite disaster.

Dear God,

As the fig tree, when productive, was a symbol of longevity, bore prized fruit, and displayed its generosity by providing shade to passersby along hot Palestinian roads, may our lives be exemplified through a variety of service, given with humility over time. May we be generous with our world's goods and human capabilities as they have been entrusted to us, even to a smile or word of encouragement. Amen.

The Parable of the Feast

Then the master said to the slave, "Go out into the roads and lanes, and compel people to come in, so that my house may be filled" (Luke 14:23).

Jesus tells of someone giving a great dinner for which he sent his slave to invite his friends. The slave returned with a litany of excuses—no one could attend.

We have seen how creatively Jesus incorporated agricultural themes into his parables. Harvests emanating from this earthly bounty materialized into feasts—religious, historical, and just plain joyful. Passover quickly comes to mind, but there was even a festival at the beginning of wheat harvest. I have read that "if two strangers met in the desert and shared a meal, an unbreakable bond was established." And further: "Guests were frequent, and ate until they rolled over on the floor, asleep." In light of this, we can begin to understand the bitter disappointment of this master when no one accepted his generous and spontaneous invitation.

Jesus had much to say about being a guest, for He often was one. He advises us on where one should properly sit at a party and who the guests should be. He leaves no feast unmentioned—wedding banquet, luncheon, dinner. In so doing, he bequeaths on us the mantle of hospitality and generosity, inferring that we put our thriftiness in our back pocket at times. Above all, he urges us to think of Him as our Heavenly Host, offering us a seat at the everlasting table of His goodness.

Dear God,
From the moment we accept Your
invitation, we are more aware that our lives are
brimming over with every good thing imaginable—
from the sun in the sky, to our families whom we
love, to the thoughts that we think, to the laughter
which unburdens our hearts. Our litany of thanks
is unending, for in You we find contentment.

In receiving these gifts, help us to creatively use them
on behalf of others; only then will our lives be the
feasts You have intended them to be. Amen.

The Parable of the Good Samaritan

"Which of these three, do you think, was neighbor to this man who fell into the hands of robbers?" He said, "The one who showed him mercy" (Luke 10:36–37).

The ancient, wealthy city of Samaria dates back to 9 B.C. Eventually, it came under the domination of several conquerors, including the Assyrians, Greeks, and Romans.

Samaritans were not historically known for being accommodating, but rather as indolent and insensitive. Despite their shared heritage with the Israelites, the Jews considered them foreigners. Even Jesus avoided traveling close by dangerous Samaritan roads.

And here we find a paradox: In Luke 17:11–19 we read that intriguing story of Jesus healing the ten Samaritan lepers, and only one returning to offer his gratefulness. We ask: Where were the other nine? However, in the parable of the Good Samaritan, if we are not familiar with the antagonistic nature between the Jews and Samaritans, it is sufficient to understand its theme in the light of offering kindness and refuge to a stranger, even when it places us at risk.

Let's call it a vignette. Enter a traveller, a priest, a Levite, and a Samaritan, each one having an excuse for passing by a man who had been robbed and beaten. The priest was concerned about usurping his laws, the Levite about the riskiness of the whole business of helping a stranger, and so on. Ah! But here's the twist! Jesus makes the "good Samaritan" the hero, the one who took pity on this half-dead man. There is salvation for all!

Dear God,
Often we misplace our loyalties, especially when
it comes to the urgent needs of others. We know
that we live in perilous times, but we also must
understand that we risk living in peril ourselves if we
ignore Your charge to care for others.
The more we learn about Jesus' time, the more
we must acknowledge that the good Samaritans
of the world lived in exceedingly dangerous
times as well; the risk is thinking about our own
well-being far too often. Help us to go beyond
ourselves for the cause of need. Amen.

The Parable of the Lost Sheep

So he told them this parable: "Which one of you, having a hundred sheep and losing one of them, does not leave the ninety-nine in the wilderness and go after the one that is lost until he finds it? When he has found it, he lays it on his shoulders and rejoices. . . . Just so, I tell you, there will be more joy in heaven over one sinner who repents than over ninety-nine righteous persons who need no repentance" (Luke 15:3–5, 7).

I am the good shepherd. The good shepherd lays down his life for the sheep (John 10:11).

Both a symbolic and literal part of both Old and New Testament life, one instantly thinks of the confident shepherd leading our hearts through Psalm 23 and the lowly shepherds who came to revel in the heavenly baby Jesus. John the Baptist introduced Jesus as the "Lamb of God."

Never a vocation meant for the faint-hearted, shepherds were by nature faithful to their sheep, even willing to lay down their lives for them. Considering the high cliffs indigenous to Biblical lands which sheep had to be tenderly guided down in order to graze in greener pastures, this characteristic was a necessity. Defenseless, sheep required constant guarding, easily falling prey to prowling animals— perhaps wolves.

Shepherds were personally accountable for every one of their sheep. Often in villages the sheep were communal property and there might be two or three shepherds in charge. When even one sheep was reported lost, the whole village was alerted. When the shepherd returned with the stray sheep astride his shoulders, everyone rejoiced.

Dear God,
It is sometimes easier for us to see when someone
we love is lost, often not wanting to admit we
are lost ourselves. We struggle alone in the deserts
of life, often too proud to turn to You for the comfort,
guidance, and love which You so tenderly give.
No matter how often we forget, we know
You always welcome us back into the gentle
folds of Your comforting arms. Amen.

Peter
St. Mary's Episcopal Church, Daytona Beach, Florida

Peter – Man of Destiny

This is but a brief glimpse of one of the most dynamic, heroic, and gifted models of Christianity. We are handicapped at best, since Peter's complex and magnificent contributions remain unrefined in this limited context. No wonder he was "first."

In attempting to draw this verbal portrait of Peter as faithfully as possible, certain differences arise between older and newer, or perhaps even revisionist, studies. The Gospel of Matthew, regarded as not only the most historically correct but beautifully organized of the gospels, is also the one containing several narratives in which the major role Peter plays can be found. I confess that Peter's impact on me was profound, and that might be because I suppose I held him in some kind of mental bondage through the years because of his denial of Jesus. A closer look is revelatory.

In the *Oxford Illustrated History of Christianity*, John McManners claims that "a work of art has an instantaneous impact," and that art can "bridge the gap between cultures with a single gesture. . . ." When one studies Peter and then explores the renderings of the golden brushes belonging to artists depicting him, herein lies a visual journey to be treasured. Peter has inspired the hands of no less than Michelangelo, Rembrandt, and Nicolas Poussin—to name only a few. They chose Peter's martyrdom, his denial, and Christ handing the keys to Saint Peter, respectively, as their subjects. Rembrandt's everyday details are to be especially savored. For the strength of his convictions alone, Peter deserves a second look!

Peter—First Among the Twelve

When they had finished breakfast, Jesus said to Simon Peter, "Simon, son of John, do you love me more than these?" He said to him, "Yes, Lord; you know that I love you." Jesus said to him, "Feed my lambs." . . . After this, he said to him, "Follow me" (John 21:1, 19).

Already a committed disciple of John the Baptist, Peter, a young fisherman, was to become the leader of the men with whom Jesus chose to live His brief days of glory and trial on this earth. He was the one we would remember for his denial of Jesus, before we remember that he would be given the power to cure the sick. Yet he was one of the great examples of the New Testament, ranking alongside Paul, in his exquisite humanness. We know him as a fisherman and disciple. We may need to be reminded that Jesus called Peter a "rock," and that two of the New Testament letters are accredited to him. During his lifetime, he traveled extensively in his efforts to establish the early Christian church.

Described as "brash," "impatient," and "complex," he was also "rock-like" and "passionate." Artistic depictions of Peter reflect a face etched with courage and strength, passion and disappointment. Peter's life would become manna to artists, strewn as it was with such sadness and dignity.

Peter is called by three names: Simon, his given name; Simeon, the original Hebrew form; and Peter, the name given him by Jesus. We have also heard the name Cephas, meaning "rock," and Jona meaning "dove," certainly two polar-opposite names to describe his nature. He is most often called Simon Peter in the Bible. We are told that Jesus' first words to Peter were, "Follow me," and that they were also His last after the resurrection.

Dear God,
Forgive us when we freeze our opinion of someone,
and fail to recognize their willingness to change.
Help us, rather, to cheer new promise
and encourage it. Amen.

Learning to Change

He went up the mountain and called to him those whom he wanted, and they came to him. And he appointed twelve, whom he also named apostles, to be with him, and to be sent out to proclaim the message . . . So he appointed the twelve: Simon (to whom he gave the name Peter) . . . (Mark 3:13–14, 16).

Named first on every apostolic list, along with James and John, this trio constituted Jesus' inner circle. A Galilean, Peter lived in Capernaum, and his home (for he was married) is thought to have been Jesus' headquarters when he was in that area.

A principal character in every gospel, Peter's life became entwined with Jesus' life and ministry. He asked the question each of us still grapples with—how many times should we forgive another? Peter witnessed mystical-like moments with Jesus that only a few could share. One of these was accompanying Jesus when a leader of the synagogue begged Jesus to restore life to his twelve-year-old daughter, a healing Jesus considered so private that he allowed only Peter, along with James and John, to accompany him. Again with James and John, Peter witnessed Jesus' transfiguration. Here the dazed, but ever-ready activist fashioned an elaborate, albeit fantastical idea: "Lord, it is good for us to be here . . . if you wish I will make three dwellings. . . ." But Jesus commanded them to "tell no one" what they had witnessed. Such sacred training!

Dear God,
How difficult it is to follow, learn, witness,
and remain silent whenever it is necessary.
We lose our patience, if not our way. We want to
wriggle free of new responsibilities we don't
understand immediately. We don't want to be tested,
we don't want things to change and we often
don't even like surprises which come with
unknown endings. Keep our minds and hearts ripe
for learning or for coping with changes in our lives.
You always accompany us through
channels of change, and we ask that You forgive us
when we question those trying passages in life. Amen.

Questions Asked; Truth Denied

But Peter said to him, "Explain this parable to us." Then he said, ". . . whatever goes into the mouth enters the stomach, and goes out into the sewer. . . . But what comes out of the mouth proceeds from the heart, and this is what defiles . . ." (Matt. 15:15, 17–18).

Now Peter was sitting outside in the courtyard. A servant girl came to him and said, "You also were with Jesus the Galilean." But he denied it before all of them, saying, "I do not know what you are talking about" (Matt. 26:69–70).

*P*erhaps it is not that Peter was so complex, but that he was so human that makes his history a perfect study! As we travel along with Peter, we can sense, more than with any other disciple, what that experience was really like, for his reactions probably express what ours might have been—had we been there. Two examples show that the behavior of the man who frequently asked difficult questions was anything but forthright when posed with difficult questions himself.

In the first example, we have the inquisitive, outspoken Peter; this was the Peter who also asked Jesus to explain the parable of the fig tree, only to notice later that the fig tree had "withered." In the doing, he elicits one of Jesus' most beloved responses in the matter of prayer (Mark 11:20–25).

In the second example, we learn that Peter the Inquirer turned into Peter-Who-Denied Jesus, the story we most associate with him. When reading the entire narrative (Matt: 26:69–75) our black feelings for Peter nearly overwhelm the message he so fiercely carried forth, both before and after Jesus' resurrection. At this moment, it must have seemed to the *reflective* Peter—for he had to be reflective to have asked the range of difficult questions which popped into his head—that he could never salvage his soul from this desperate, dehumanizing act. Perhaps he even believed that the salvation that Jesus had promised could never be his. Luke tells us, however, that Jesus "appeared to Simon" after His resurrection, Jesus showing not only divine compassion towards Peter, but also personal concern for this most special disciple.

Dear God,
How we must weary You with all of our faults,
tryings, and founderings! How often we need
Your gentle encouragement to help us forgive
ourselves—let alone ask for Your forgiveness—for
the unnecessary ways we offend, ignore, or minimize
someone else's needs—and often even our own.
Help us also, Dear God, to acknowledge the good
in ourselves, the side of us that does try
to help others and be aware of their needs. Amen.

Witness to the Revelation

He asked his disciples, "Who do people say that the Son of Man is?" And they said, "Some say John the Baptist, but others Elijah. . . ." He said to them, "But who do you say that I am?" Simon Peter answered, "You are the Messiah, the Son of the living God." And Jesus answered him, "Blessed are you, Simon, son of Jonah. For flesh and blood has not revealed this to you, but my Father in heaven" (Matt. 16:13–17).

Come to him, a living stone, though rejected by mortals, yet chosen and precious in God's sight, and like living stones, let yourselves be built into a spiritual house, to be a holy priesthood . . . (1 Pet. 2:4).

The first exchange between Jesus and Peter did not take place soon after Peter had met Jesus; rather it occurred after Peter had seen Jesus in many different situations: the telling of the parables, performing miracles, or even breaking laws on the Sabbath. Peter, by this time, had seen Jesus in a myriad of situations, and he must have wondered and reflected upon just who Jesus was. That he was given the gift which enabled him to discern Jesus' true identity at an especially difficult historical time of doubt and confusion is an indication that Peter had learned to trust Jesus unequivocally.

Jesus' words, spoken to Peter just after he stated his belief that Jesus was the Messiah, have led to many interpretations. But Peter himself seems intent on explaining his interpretation of what they meant by carrying the metaphor of the rock into words attributed to him in 1 Peter. We are not a rock, but "living stones," and in Peter 1:2, we are charged to follow in Jesus' steps. Jesus should be the foundation stone of our life, Peter tells us in his own definitive way. And certainly Peter's faith could be another metaphor for a rock-like element on which Jesus' church could be built.

Dear God,
The younger Peter seems to have possessed
nearly every negative human characteristic we can
imagine. Still, look how Jesus understood Peter
and loved him, despite all of his inconsistencies.

And yet, the mature Peter admonishes us to let
ourselves "be built into a spiritual house"—his way
of telling us to keep our hearts, souls, and bodies
free of as much of the debris of life as possible.
And lead us not into temptation. Amen.

A Charge to Keep

And I tell you, you are Peter, and on this rock I will build my church and the gates of Hades will not prevail against it. I will give you the keys of the kingdom of heaven, and whatever you bind on earth will be bound in heaven . . . (Matt. 16:18–19).

How did Peter go about keeping Jesus' charge? Given his record, one could imagine that after Jesus' ascension, he would be anxious to go home and perhaps spend some time with his family. However, Peter's documented activities in the days after Christ make the hairs rise on the back of one's neck. With sheer deliberativeness and fearlessness, he seemed intent on not failing again.

Listen to his achievements: Declaring that Jesus had been freed from death by God "because it was impossible for him to be held in its power" (Acts 2:14–42), Peter preached the first Christian sermon. With John, the Beloved Disciple, Peter healed the lame man at the gate of the temple (Acts 3:1–10). Traveling extensively in his successful efforts to establish the Christian church, it was Peter, amidst voracious criticism, who forced the doors of the early church to open to Gentiles. (Just imagine those turbulent times—the overturning of ancient Jewish beliefs.) Even Paul acknowledges Peter's astonishing leadership and equality, reminding us that Peter had been "entrusted with the gospel for the circumcised" (Gal. 2), just as he (Paul) had been entrusted with the uncircumcised. Peter was not given to dwelling on the mistakes of yesterday; he had a charge to keep, and he kept it!

Dear God,

When we allow our responsibilities to weigh us down, they do. Often we make matters worse by harboring guilt about things we think we ought to have done, but didn't. We can even be very creative in justifying our anxieties, but not delight in our achievements. Even worse, we linger endlessly on the mistakes of a tarnished yesterday.

Help us instead to focus on the newness and forgiveness of each day You grant us. Only then can we fully realize the unique "us" which resides in each of our hearts. Amen.

Peter's Legacy in Acts and Letters

Then Peter began to speak to them: "I truly understand that God shows no partiality, but in every nation anyone who fears him and does what is right is acceptable to him. You know the message he sent to the people of Israel, preaching peace by Jesus Christ—he is Lord of all" (Acts 10:34–36).

Above all, maintain constant love for one another, for love covers a multitude of sins. Be hospitable to one another without complaining. Like good stewards of the manifold grace of God, serve one another with whatever gift each of you has received (1 Pet. 4:8–10).

*P*eter's role in the creation of the Christian church is related in the first half of Acts; thereafter, the focus is on Paul. As for Peter, we are not surprised to learn that as he became a leader in establishing the church, he began delivering fiery, powerful sermons. It was through Cornelius, a Roman soldier who sought God's message, however, that Peter realized that no one should be prevented from joining the fledgling Christian community. Inviting fury among the Jews, Peter baptized him. Throughout Acts 1–15, Peter's life and experiences, eventually leading to martyrdom, is told. If you are looking for adventure, the perils of the persecuted, the light of a visionary truth, a powerful message, and some inspirational passages, Luke's book of Acts conveys it all!

While a few sources believe that Peter is the actual author of the two letters—or extended sermons, as some would say—bearing his name, most scholars attribute them otherwise, and for various reasons. The intricacies of scholarship are of infinite interest, of course; however, in this brief study of Peter, we are more in need of encouragement to live our lives as God commands us. Here we have hit a gusher, for the letters attributed to Peter advise on leadership, living, and loving through perilous times, while trusting in God through it all. Encouragement for any and all times of our lives!

Dear God,
We know that You have given us lively spirits, which,
if we are so inclined, lead us ever closer to You.
And yet, we also know that You have given us free
will, the desire to create life each in our unique way.
You have urged us along separate paths
of achievement, reconciliation, and purpose.
There is, we admit, a Peter-like character in each of us.

At whatever stage of life we happen to find ourselves,
because we have chosen to follow You, we do indeed
experience the whole realm of life: happiness and
frustration, stability and disruption, disillusion and joy,
periods of creativity and times of lackluster. And yet we
have learned from many of those we have studied from
Your word, and as Peter's life has revealed, that we can
continue to contribute to our own well-being and
the well-being of others when we remove barriers of
self-flagellation and remember our humanness.

Help us to meet the challenges of life with grace, to savor the
good moments, and to gratefully acknowledge Your gentle
love for us, even when our dreams falter, for this is the only
way we can be all that You have intended us to be. Amen.

Jesus with Mary and Martha
St. Cross by the Sea Episcopal Church, Hermosa Beach, California

New Testament Testimonies

ollowing are glimpses of nine dedicated New Testament participants to the before, then, and thereafter world that marked Christ's birth, life, and resurrection. They include Christ's mother, Mary; Elizabeth and Zechariah; John the Baptist; Martha; Simon of Cyrene; Stephen; and Priscilla and Aquila. I have also included a personal reflection on Jesus.

These were not easy choices to make, for the New Testament is overflowing with men and women who came from all avenues of life professionally and from varying economic circumstances. Each heard a long-hoped for message and responded to it with vigor and imagination, probably using talents they never thought theirs.

The New Testament is less than one-third as long as its more ancient counterpart, the Old Testament. Compiled within a century after Jesus' death, the New Testament consists of twenty-seven books. Despite probing over the centuries, the authorship of several books or letters remains in doubt. Still, "No other message has been read by as many people in as many tongues, over as long a period of time, as this 'literature of a mission.'"

Christ's Mother, Mary

But Mary treasured all these words and pondered them in her heart (Luke 2:19).

This, my favorite verse from childhood, has remained so, even though I could not have possibly understood much about its significance then. Mary's esteemed place as Jesus' mother remains the unsurpassed example of motherhood and, indeed, womanhood. So little is still known of her, it is tempting to fill in the gaps with our own sentimentality. Still, what *do* we know of her?

Remember how, after being informed that she, unwed, was to give birth to the long-awaited Messiah, Mary sought the support of her older cousin, Elizabeth? Might we not have sought the same kind of comfort? We can imagine how she must have lovingly encouraged Jesus, but we know that neither did she hesitate to admonish her twelve-year-old for straying from his parents—and we certainly understand the anxiety she experienced. Mary, as well, has the distinction of having been the only one to be with Jesus not only at his birth but also at his death. What misery Mary must have known, there at the foot of her son's cross; she must have been frozen with sadness. However, even as we may wish to think we would respond as Mary did, she remains an uncompromising inspiration for each of us.

And so, in a word, "ponder"—or to "think deeply" as *Webster's Dictionary* defines it—tells us much of what we need to know about her. And by telling us these things were in her heart, Luke tells us she not only thought deeply, but felt deeply. All of this helps us understand why such a seemingly "ordinary" woman was chosen by God to nurture the treasure of treasures we know and love as Jesus.

Dear God,
The sheen of motherhood—and womanhood—never
glows more affirmatively than at Christmastime.
We know that You understand how we can struggle
with the everydayness of raising, teaching,
and guiding our children, even as You patiently
love and understand us. Amen.

Elizabeth and Zechariah

Both of them were righteous before God, living blamelessly according to all the commandments and regulations of the Lord. But they had no children, because Elizabeth was barren, and both were getting on in years (Luke 1:6–7).

Zechariah and Elizabeth—now there was a marriage made in heaven! We are made immediately aware of their importance in that we are introduced to Zechariah almost immediately in Luke's thoughtful retelling of Jesus' birth, Elizabeth soon thereafter. They symbolize the patience, forbearance, and love that must be woven into any marriage, despite their deep cultural and personal disappointment of having had no children. They also possessed the attributes of personal holiness necessary to accomplish God's plan. However, we are also reminded that God's hand touched each of them individually; each was given an incalculably important role to play. There they were in their old age when the angel Gabriel appeared to Zechariah giving him the startling message that Elizabeth would bear a son named John. Elizabeth, with great joy and dignity, bore him.

Dear God,
Help us not to pretend we can ordain our own
destiny. Our hearts tell us that by carefully
cultivating our own spiritual gifts, we can live
our lives most fully when we invite You to walk
our daily path with us. Sometimes we actually
convince ourselves that we have no time to listen
to our spiritual selves, for being in control
of what we think are our own lives is something
the chatter of the world encourages.

This beloved Bible story teaches us, in part, that
Your messages are often an adventure veiled in
treasures beyond our comprehension. It also teaches
us that our lives always matter and in perhaps
surprising ways, whatever our stage—or age.
Help us always to be attentive to Your subtle ways,
for we may be chosen ourselves to serve You
at some least expected time. Amen.

John the Baptist

All who heard them [Zechariah and Elizabeth] *pondered them and said, "What then will this child become?" For, indeed, the hand of the Lord was with him (Luke 1:66).*

What a friend (and relative) Jesus had in John! Loyal, fearless, straightforward in word and deed, he was brought into the world for the most sacred purpose—to announce the coming of Jesus Christ. With Elizabeth and Zechariah as his parents, we know that John was surely "trained" in the way he should go, and that he never departed from it.

Setting himself apart from the noise of more enlightened city life, John chose to live in a natural, compatible-to-him environment, a choice we might have considered odd then, despite our interest and emphasis on environmental concerns in the present. It is clear that Jesus and John shared a complete and loving understanding of each other's respective missions.

What an unselfish, infectious spirit he must have had! We know of John's ultimate punishment by the hand of Herod, but surely the days when he walked freely about the desert, finding contentment in the surrounding waters, baptizing believers from any persuasion, and awaiting the Messiah, were the memories he carried with him unto death. Of eternal importance, John was the fulfiller of Old Testament prophecy through the long ago promises of Old Testament prophets, Isaiah and Malachi.

Dear God,
John was so exemplary. From him, we learn both
simplicities—like not making quick judgments because of
someone's outward appearance—and complexities—
like the fact that unbridled faith brings
the ultimate gift of peace. Thank You for John's
holiness and the rich sparseness of his everyday life.
In other words, thank You for one who personified
a life which peeled away unnecessary layers,
but still found contentment in discovering
how silken life can really be. Amen.

Martha

Now as they went on their way, he entered a certain village, where a woman named Martha welcomed him into her home. She had a sister named Mary, who sat at the Lord's feet and listened to what he was saying. But Martha was distracted by her many tasks . . . (Luke 10:38–40).

*I*magine being Martha and living in a culture which honored hospitality! Jesus was coming for dinner! Martha might have thought: *Jesus has been traveling; he doesn't get many homecooked meals; I know what he likes and I'll prepare it for him.* Mary probably thought: *Jesus can't visit that often. I'll just sit here and listen to Him speak.* In the presence of her sister, Martha became a tool for comparison. It is easy to judge or misjudge her, but perhaps we need to give her a bit more understanding. In reality, I think she is more like many of us than we would like to admit. How often have we complained because someone "just doesn't do a thing" or "leaves all of the work for someone else to do"? In our time, we might call Martha an activist and would not mean it derisively at all. But we might admit we have allowed the details of life to set the stage!

Jesus settled this sibling argument without leaving any question as to which one had chosen correctly. In Martha's case, the last time she is mentioned, she is once again serving a meal to Jesus and his disciples, but in silence. We know she was listening!

Dear God,
Once again we come asking that You help us find
that slippery balance in life. Help us to sort life out,
to know what is appropriate for the happy times,
as well as for the inevitable trials which can flood
our own lives. Help us ask what Jesus would do.
And then give us the wisdom to come as close as
we can to behaving with our hearts, minds,
and emotions in thoughtful balance. Amen.

Simon of Cyrene

They compelled a passer-by, who was coming in from the country, to carry his cross; it was Simon of Cyrene (Mark 15:21).

*P*icture this. You have come from another country and are on your way to a celebration. Suddenly, a soldier taps you on the shoulder and makes you part of the most tragic scene in history. In this case, the passer-by is Simon of Cyrene who, having travelled from Africa, was on his way to Passover when he suddenly found himself pressed into service and asked to carry Jesus' cross to Golgotha—the place of the skulls.

Do you think he probably thought his holiday was ruined? Usually when someone was convicted of a crime and sentenced to hang on the cross—common in those days—the accused was forced to carry his own cross. For Jesus an exception was made. It is Barclay who conjectures that the experience must have led to one of the finest conversions of all time. There are two pieces of supporting evidence: first, Simon is mentioned as the father of Rufus and Alexander. It is Paul, in one of his many exuberant greetings which helps us keep track of people, who also mentions Rufus and his mother, who would have been Simon's wife. We may infer that what Simon experienced that day must have led to his conversion as he took back home with him the story of that riveting experience.

Dear God,

Increase our awareness of life to new experiences and adventures that are most often found in service to others. We learn through Simon that they can often be paths to Christian growth we never could have expected. You lived Your life as a model for us, but at this time and at this place known as Golgotha, You were the supreme example of love made perfect.

We struggle with carrying the smallest of crosses in our own lives, forgetting that we never need carry the full weight of any cross alone. Amen.

Stephen

Stephen, full of grace and power, did great wonders and signs among the people. But they could not withstand the wisdom and the Spirit with which he spoke. Then they secretly instigated some men to say, "We have heard him speak blasphemous words against Moses and God" (Acts 6:8, 10–11).

A Christian model for all time, Stephen translated his life into an everlasting testimony for Christ. A steward of the earliest of churches, he was a gifted man in many respects, who, despite being a powerful orator and administrator, was also involved in the daily distribution of food to the poor. A most trusted officer in the earliest of churches, there were those jealous of his wisdom and knowledge who brought charges against him. In defending himself before the Sanhedrin, or "supreme court of chief priests and elders in Jerusalem," Stephen delivered a speech recounting the history of the Jews, dating back to their earliest ancestry, and urging them to accept the reality of who Jesus was. The ultimate effect was a dispersal of the church beyond Jerusalem to other communities.

His persecution ultimately came by stoning, with Paul (then Saul) participating, an experience which led directly to Paul's later conversion. To know that such a one as Stephen existed is to know that God's hand is ever-guiding and knowing, and reminds us of the unmined potential in each one of us.

Dear God,

Stephen was molded of every noble human quality for which we could ever hope. He revealed to us an inner spirit, alive and working within him, which he did not try in the least to deny. Yet he seems very real to us. Through his example, may we redefine our spirituality with ever more clarity and rethink how You want us to use it. Give us, then, the necessary determination, character, and love so that our lives will make a shared difference. Amen.

Priscilla and Aquila

Greet Priscilla and Aquila, who work with me in Christ Jesus, and who risked their necks for my life . . . (Romans 16:3–4).

Barclay believed that "there is no more fascinating pair of people in the New Testament than Priscilla and Aquila." My Bible refers to them as "exciting new leaders." We know that they were Jews who lived in Rome, but that Claudius had issued an edict in A.D. 52 banishing the Jews. They met Paul in Corinth when he was on his second journey, eventually developing such a valued friendship that Paul lived with them.

We know that Priscilla and Aquila had become Christians before they met Paul, and were among its early teachers. They shared the lucrative occupation of tent making with Paul, and when he left for Ephesus, they followed. A most wealthy and cosmopolitan place, Paul established one of the strongest churches there. They led a curiously nomadic life, also accompanying Paul to Syria before they returned to Rome. Their home, wherever it was, was always open to Christian fellowship. Aquila and Priscilla are also credited with instructing the converted orator, Apollos, who was himself said to be a great teacher.

Dear God,
May we offer to You not only the openness of
our hearts, but the openness of our homes. May they
be havens of hospitality and comfort for others.

Thank You for inspirations like Priscilla and Aquila.
Their examples are easy ones for us to understand.
They highlight for us the most loving proof of a
marriage illuminated by your radiating beam
of light. They exhibited, as well, the courageous
zeal for life which is so appealing to those who
would call themselves Christians. Amen.

Jesus

Do not let your hearts be troubled. Believe in God, believe also in me (John 14:1).

*D*uring Lent, I heard someone sing that hallowed hymn "I Walked Today Where Jesus Walked," a hymn that fills my heart with a flight of imagination. This song made me realize how through my lifetime my love for Jesus has been enriched through music. The words of a hymn can fill one's spirit to overflowing with all that being a Christian can mean. Remembering my childhood when I stood alongside my mother in church, my arm folded through hers, we sang those sweet hymns of devotion like "In the Garden," "Ivory Palaces," and "I Would Be True." But it was probably in daily vacation Bible school that I first learned "Into My Heart." Do you know it? It is an invitation to know Jesus' immeasurable love:

> Into my heart,
> Into my heart,
> Come into my heart, Lord Jesus.
> Come in today, come in to stay.
> Come into my heart, Lord Jesus.

He did, of course, and He has!

Dear God,

Surely one of the happiest childhood memories we possess is remembering songs we were taught in Sunday School. They were mostly songs of joy then, but as we grew, we learned hymns of praise, holiness, and comfort. Fragments of them often flow through our minds without a hint of notice, but just in time to inflate our hearts at our most celebratory moments or relieve our fears when they overwhelm us.

We slowly understand that music has no emotional or denominational boundaries. How often we have anticipated the second we collectively rise to the first note of the "Hallelujah" chorus. I have sung a song unknown to me until a few years ago, when I grieved the loss of mutual friends at a Catholic Mass. Here a hymn assured me that one day I may be lifted up "on eagle's wings." The whole experience amounted to a soaring sound and promise of salvation I cannot forget. For which I thank You.

And, Lord, we know that You sought the solace of a hymn after the Last Supper . . . for the Bible tells us so. Amen.

Stephen
Redeemer Lutheran Church, Lincoln, Nebraska

A Little Journey with Paul

Paul's overarching message was that his conversion was truly of a divine nature, coming as it did directly from God.

As we know, Paul was of Jewish heritage, having been born circa A.D. 10 to 15, in Tarsus. His father was a Roman citizen and assumed to be of some means since later in his life, Paul was allowed to go to Rome for his trial. He was educated in Jerusalem by the famous teacher, Gamaliel, but became a zealist nationalist and probably a Pharisee. This was the Jewish sect which clung to scrupulous observations that governed the everyday life of a Jew. He was believed to have been a tentmaker, but became known as the "church's first theologian."

Paul is a perfect study for us. He had a world view; he also had personal affliction, a "thorn in the side" with which many of us can associate. He also traveled widely on behalf of Christ. Of course, Paul wrestled with his belief as we often do. In this case, however, he disappeared into the Arabian desert for several years after his conversion in order to prepare for his missionary life. This kind of early dedication became one of Paul's most defining hallmarks.

It was the brutality of which he himself was a part—Stephen being stoned—which set him upon the road to Christianity. At the time of his stunning conversion, he was actually traveling to Damascus to put down the spread of Christianity there. We will pick up Paul's story as he begins his first missionary excursion.

As we embark on this journey with Paul, Dear God, may we find a place within ourselves to begin anew, just as Paul did.

Travels, Choices

But when the Jews saw the crowds, they were filled with jealousy; and blaspheming, they contradicted what was spoken by Paul. Then both Paul and Barnabas spoke out boldly, saying, "It was necessary that the word of God should be spoken first to you. Since you reject it and judge yourselves to be unworthy of eternal life, we are now turning to the Gentiles . . ." (Acts 13:45–46).

The book of Acts, written by Luke, is the link between Christ's life and the life of the Church, Paul having been the central artery in the formation of the early Church. It chronicles in some detail Paul's journeys. Setting out first for Cyprus, Paul traveled with Barnabas, who was a converted Levite, and the youthful John Mark, who, as he matured, gave us the gift of the Gospel of Mark.

Paul's travels were critical to the formation of the early Church, which required someone of his persistence and communicative skills. His blinding experience along the road to Damascus led to his baptism, but also to convictions of tremulous dimension.

During his lifetime, Paul undertook four journeys, always with trusted companions. Traveling by foot and by sea, and beginning circa A.D. 46, Cyprus, Asia Minor, Macedonia, Greece, Ephesus, and Syria were among the places he visited and set foundations for the early church. On his way to Jerusalem, he was arrested, "ultimately taken to Rome," and put on trial A.D. 62.

One of the foremost problems of the early church was that of converting the Jews. It became Peter's task to do that, while the conversion of the Gentiles became Paul's central mission.

Dear God,
The early Christians and the establishment of the
Church we have come to love mean ever more to us.
We realize they struggled with serious dissension in
establishing an institution without a smidgen of a
foundation, which became their legacy to us
centuries later. We thank You especially for
Paul's encouragement and we ask that You let our
minds feel free to wander back over the dusty
roads he traveled, speaking his heart for
Christ's sake. Amen.

An Inspired "First"

Then certain individuals came down from Judea and were teaching the brothers. "Unless you are circumcised according to the custom of Moses, you cannot be saved.". . . Paul and Barnabas . . . were appointed to go up to Jerusalem to discuss the question with the apostles and elders . . . (Acts 15:1–11).

$\mathcal{P}$aul knew in his heart that while taking Christianity to the Gentiles would not be easy, a real stumbling block would be whether or not they should have to adhere to the laws of Moses and other Jewish traditions. Most troubling was the problem of circumcision. He knew his success among the Gentiles would be limited unless he could help free them of this cultural hindrance.

Naturally, this generated a heated discussion which ended in a religious stalemate. Paul traveled to Jerusalem to appear before the Council of Jerusalem (meeting there with Peter and James), to make this transforming plea. This meeting is considered the first ecumenical meeting in the history of Christianity. Imagine the moment these powerful orators made this astonishing request, in the end actually persuading the council that converts should not have to be circumcised. This remained one of Paul's most critical themes: salvation through faith, not laws.

Dear God,
Thank You for the gift of interpretation which
came through Paul. It enables us to avoid a
labyrinth of justification for our decision to know
You as a personal friend and guide. "Faith through
salvation" is a gift like no other and renders
Paul's contributions golden scepters of truth.

Thank You also for the faith of all those who have
gone before us, who helped lead us down this path
of love. Our mothers and fathers, pastors, and true
friends who share and shared with us
this glowing beam of light in our own lives. Amen.

Paul – A Man For All Seasons

They asked only one thing, that we remember the poor, which was actually what I was eager to do (Gal. 2:10).

Paul? At Christmastime? Why not!? Paul, zealous in all he did, never minced words. Remembering the poor, of course, was a constant theme in New Testament theology.

We are aware of Paul's many letters to the churches that he helped to establish. Fourteen New Testament letters are traditionally attributed to him; however, only seven, Galatians being one of them, are accepted without doubt as authentically Paul's writing. In them we find familiar and needed themes of encouragement, caring for the poor, and—resoundingly—believing in the Spirit! Educated as he was, Paul's letters have become the purest examples of Greek writing.

Paul could not resist personalizing the last part of this verse. As Christians we can personalize the meaning of poor to fit others' needs as we see them—in health, in spirit, or in providing the means to allow someone to maintain the sanctity of their own dignity. The candles we light on Christmas Eve will burn ever brighter if we can claim one "extra" outreach every Christmas as our very own. Just a smidgen of Paul's dedication and eagerness will go a long way, in fact, at any season of the year!

Dear God,
As if it weren't enough that You sent us the miracle
of Jesus, You also sent us Paul. He helps us lift the
life of Jesus into brighter focus by enthusiastically
delving into Christ's full significance—at least as
much as any human being could.

Here he encourages us to remember the poor, but in
our hearts we know that the word "poor" has
connotations which can range from a surprise
invitation to dinner to a lonely friend, to listening
to the unburdening of a broken heart—if and when
we can. At such times, perhaps we can ourselves open
the door to the mystery of happiness which comes as
we contribute small gifts of this nature to others.
All, of course, in Jesus' name. Amen.

Every Soul Matters

On the sabbath day we went outside the gate by the river, where we supposed there was a place of prayer; . . . A certain woman named Lydia, a worshipper of God, was listening to us; . . . The Lord opened her heart to listen eagerly to what was said by Paul. When she and her household were baptized, she urged us, saying, "If you have judged me to be faithful to the Lord, come and stay at my home." And she prevailed upon us (Acts 16:13–15).

*P*aul, diverted from his plans as so often happened (this time by a vision from God), arrived in Philippi. A sign over the "arches" to the city forbade the teaching of any "unrecognized religion." It was, therefore, outside the city limits where he met Lydia, a successful businesswoman who sold purple cloth, a favored color worn by royalty.

Lydia and several other women were meeting there. After hearing Paul speak, in what has been recorded as Paul's "first evangelistic contact with a small group of women," while others considered Paul's invitation to Christian baptism, Lydia immediately accepted. Apparently, Lydia was a woman who knew her mind as well as her heart, which might, wouldn't you agree, account for much of her success! This gave her the historical distinction of being "Paul's first European convert." Inviting Paul to stay at her home thereafter, her hospitality ranks among the most authentic of Christian attributes. One source enhances her documented status by asserting that "Lydia's house later became the first church in Philippi."

One-by-one or by the score, the passion with which Paul preached his message of Jesus' love continues to change history, even unto today.

Dear God,
There was such momentum in Paul's life; his
pace makes us wonder if we ever really accomplish
anything. Yet we know that each humble
contribution we make with You in our hearts is one
that You cherish and understand. Help us
to always seek times when we can soften the edges
of someone else's life even a trifle. Amen.

Making a Joyful Noise

About midnight Paul and Silas were praying and singing hymns to God, and the prisoners were listening to them. Suddenly there was an earthquake so violent that . . . all the doors were opened and everyone's chains unfastened . . . (Acts 16:25–26).

Silas was another of Paul's traveling companions and true friends. He was with Paul when the pair was stripped, beaten, whipped, and thrown into prison. And so we learn what real spirit is when we read that they were "praying and singing hymns" under these circumstances.

Timothy was another who accompanied Paul on his second and third journeys. Paul praised him soundly when he wrote of Timothy, "I have no one like him who will be genuinely concerned for your welfare . . ."

Luke, of course, was not only the author of the book named for him, but of Acts as well. He was also considered a most trusted and faithful companion for Paul.

And so, whatever trials awaited Paul, God did grant him the gift of enduring friendships—God-given friends who stayed with Paul through those often sudden and difficult storms in his life.

Dear God,
Thank You for the gift of friendship. It comes
to us in sometimes quiet, sometimes exciting,
and—at times—the most difficult of periods in our
lives. Help us to recognize and cherish it.
Help us to show others what their friendship
means to us by extending ourselves
in special times of someone else's need.
We can also be the anchors that others are for us.
You, of course, are our constant Friend
and the centerpiece of our lives. Amen.

Acceptance

Then Paul answered, "What are you doing, weeping and breaking my heart? For I am ready not only to be bound but even to die in Jerusalem for the name of the Lord Jesus." Since he would not be persuaded, we remained silent except to say, "The Lord's will be done" (Acts 21:13—14).

Although Paul had planned to go to Spain, he was dedicated to returning to Jerusalem to take with him a gift of money "to symbolize the bond uniting Christians everywhere, and to make the Jewish members of the Church at Jerusalem more conscious of the love of their Gentile Christian brothers for them." He continued to teach and show by example that no Christian or Christianized Jew need follow certain aspects of Jewish law. In fact, there were now "thousands of believers" among the Jews. But Paul was eventually arrested each time riots broke out wherever he went. Finally, he was taken away by the authorities. Allowed to make a speech in his own defense, his Roman citizenship could not be questioned. However, Paul was imprisoned and ultimately spent two years at the bastille in Caesarea.

Dear God,
Paul's example is almost beyond our capacity
to understand. For You, he was willing to be arrested
repeatedly, living much of his life by accepting the
violence which was so pervasive during his lifetime.
And yet we know that he also sought the silence
of the desert and, at times, must have longed for a few
moments to himself, as many of us often do.

We cannot expect to rival Paul in any way.
We can only be eternally grateful for his
miraculous Christianhood. Amen.

Courage Without Question

I urge you now to keep up your courage, for there will be no loss of life among you, but only of the ship. For last night there stood by me an angel of the God to whom I belong . . . and he said to me, "Do not be afraid, Paul; you must stand before the emperor . . . and God has granted safety to all those who are sailing with you." So keep up your courage . . . (Acts 27:22–25).

*P*aul, however he might have known his destiny, asked not to be tried at Jerusalem and appealed to Caesar, as his Roman citizenship entitled him to do, to go to Rome where he believed he would have a more fair trial. This was granted; it was on this journey that he experienced what has been called "one of the most famous shipwreck stories of literature." (Acts 27:1–28) Upon arriving in Rome, he was given an apartment, where friends could visit him. Because he was either unknown and/or because of loss of papers due to his shipwreck, Paul spent another two years awaiting trial (A.D. 59–61). Some scholars believe that it was during this period that Paul wrote Ephesians, Philippians, Philemon, and Colossians. Often considered letters, they addressed "particular problems" in specific churches. Paul, it seems, never wasted time. Uncertainty remains as to exactly where, when, and how Paul died; however, it is generally agreed that he was beheaded before the end of A.D. 62.

Dear God,
Would that our mission in life be as clearly
defined to us as Paul's became to him. The center of
thunderstorms of every kind, he continued to trust
in Your guidance, knowing that whatever came
his way, that was the way he would go.

None of us is free of problems; quelling life's storms
has never been easy. The age in which we live is a time
of unusual disturbance in our lives. But grief, illness,
and feeling disheartened are also shared among us;
for as we know, we are all one in You and are meant to
share the misfortunes of our friends. This bond of
interconnectedness is a divine gift of Your love. Amen.

Paul and Timothy
Rye Presbyterian Church, Rye, New York

Paul and His Companions

ntended to complement *A Little Journey With Paul*, the theme of this section is to show how God masterfully provided companionship for Paul throughout his unparalled ministry.

Paul is said to have traveled 17,825 miles, the equivalent of halfway around the world. Mastermind that he was, he could not have achieved all that he did alone. We do well to explore the character of those who accompanied him on his treacherous journeys. Paul's friends, there to support him at every turn, were superior men and women.

They include Barnabas, John Mark, Philip, Luke, Eunice, Lois, Timothy, and Silas. You have met some of them before, but, beacons that they are, we would do well to spend a little time in additional exploration of these companions in Paul's life. This is a tribute to their faith and faithfulness.

As we have seen, the New Testament is overflowing with examples of healthy marriages, tested and true friendships, words of wisdom and encouragement, and stories which have helped us survive in our own time. They weave us into an eternal tapestry of love.

Barnabas

When he [Paul] had come to Jerusalem, he attempted to join the disciples; and they were all afraid of him, for they did not believe that he was a disciple. But Barnabas took him, brought him to the apostles, and described for them how on the road he had seen the Lord, who had spoken to him, and how in Damascus he had spoken boldly in the name of Jesus (Acts 9:26–27).

The question which comes to mind as one reads this action-packed passage is: What would have happened to Paul had it not been for Barnabas' explanation about the sincerity of Paul's conversion? After all, Paul had participated in the stoning of Stephen, considered to be the first Christian martyr. But here was God providing a man of courage who was willing to speak on Paul's behalf, knowing he was placing himself at risk.

Thus did Barnabas establish himself as one of the principle participants in Paul's embryonic ministry, even accompanying him on his first mission. It was he who brought the young John Mark, his nephew, to travel with Paul and himself as they began their conversion of Gentiles. Although their travels together ended when Barnabas supported John Mark despite his youthful mistakes, Barnabas remains one of the "most quietly influential people in the early days of Christianity." It is from him that we learn that encouragement can be the mortar of a destiny fulfilled.

Dear God,

We know that no one can wear those velvet robes
of kindness that are Yours alone, but we are grateful
that we have examples like Barnabas who is
remembered for his many acts of encouragement
and loyalty. Forgive us if any day of our lives
should flutter by without our having spoken
a charitable word to someone.

Even when we may not be well ourselves,
encouraging someone is a gift we can always have
at our fingertips. We really have no way of knowing
how those few words may sustain another. Amen.

John Mark

The beginning of the good news of Jesus Christ, the Son of God (Mark 1:1).

So begins the book of Mark; perhaps it is even your favorite gospel. This, the earliest of the four Gospels, is the one drawn upon by the authors of both Matthew and Luke. Story-like in form, it is told simply and honestly and with a certain inescapable enthusiasm. Many scholars believe that, although Mark was not one of the original disciples, he was, in fact, a witness to the wonders Jesus performed. The then youthful Mark managed to generate the same excitement in this fast-paced book attributed to him, obviously written some years later, and with the meat of it supplied by Peter. We pray that we may retain some of Mark's youthful enthusiasm ourselves!

He is, of course, the same Mark chosen by his uncle, Barnabas, to accompany Paul and him on their first missionary journey. Youthful to a distracting degree, Paul refused to allow him to continue as he prepared for his second journey. This caused such friction between Paul and Barnabas (who, characteristically, took up Mark's cause), that it is believed that they never traveled together again.

Barnabas and Mark, however, embarked on a missionary journey of their own. We know that these trips were in themselves responsible for the conversion of many and, therefore, part of God's plan. Years later, when Paul was imprisoned, he requested Mark's presence, a supreme illustration of forgiveness in action—in both directions. We know, however, that the forgiver is always the primary beneficiary at such times.

Mark is the shortest of the gospels, but its chronological narrative gives us a straight-forward account of Jesus' days of ministry on earth.

Dear God,
Wherever would we be without Mark's eyewitness
accounts of Jesus' faithful journey? Through him
we know of Your constant and continuing love for us,
and of the healing love at Your fingertips. Amen.

Philip

*The crowds with one accord listened eagerly to what was said by Philip,
hearing and seeing the signs that he did . . . So there was great joy in the
city (Acts 8:6, 8).*

There were several Philips who lived in Biblical times;
here we speak of one known as "Philip the Evangelist."
He bears the distinction of having been chosen with
Stephen as one of the original seven deacons of the Church.
These seven were assigned to distribute food to the widows
of the Greeks; thereby ministering not only to women in
need, but going beyond the boundaries of the Christian
community. Philip was, therefore, among the first
missionaries. Christ's message had become his lifeline and
he eventually traveled to nations which might not have
heard of Christ's love otherwise.

Traveling outside of Jerusalem, he went to Samaria, a
near-forbidden land for Jews; the desert of Ethiopia, where
he converted the Ethiopian prince to Christianity; and also
to Caesarea, where he was Paul's host in the last years before
Paul's imprisonment. A follower, a believer, a missionary, a
visionary, one who cared for the indigent, and a gentle man,
Philip may well be thought of as "Philip the Inspirer." His
legacy of caring for and distributing food to those in need is
one that continues to be carried out by those whose loving
presence we are privileged to know even today.

Dear God,
We have little excuse to be other than You would
have us be. In Philip, we gain even deeper insight
into how You would have us live our lives, how You
would have us mold our time here on earth. Acts of
kindness, acts of faith, acts of worship, and acts of
hospitality—all these elixirs shine brightly in the
character of Philip. And so may they in us,
according to our own strengths. Amen.

Luke

Only Luke is with me (2 Tim. 4:11).

This fragment of Paul's writings allows us to see Luke, the author of the third gospel, as the compassionate physician and friend that he was. In this despairing moment, Paul was facing his life's end alone, *except for Luke,* who remained to ease his mind and body. Is this not a story to treasure? History records Paul, for all his activity, as often being in ill-health (remember that "thorn in his side"?), so having Luke to care for him must have been of great consolation, surely an act of God.

Luke, a Gentile, was also a historian. His gospel was directed at his own people, his mission to show Jesus as the most human of human beings. His book is considered the "most comprehensive" of the gospels. Also recognized as the author of Acts, both books are counted as "reliable, historical documents." We can only imagine how his emphasis on Jesus' humanity influenced Paul's understanding, as well as the direction of what eventually became Paul's dynamic and influential church doctrine.

Dear God,
Sometimes taken for granted are those who
support us in our weaker times, those who
care enough for us to listen to our problems,
or even ease the monotony of every-day life
by visiting us, or showing even a wisp of attention
to us. Is it not these people who hold heaven's gates
within their grasp because they understand
the difference that their caring can make
to another's well being? Help us to recognize
these seemingly smaller gifts and gratefully return
them whenever we sense their need. Amen.

Eunice and Lois

I am reminded of your sincere faith, a faith that lived first in your grandmother Lois and your mother Eunice and, now, I am sure, lives in you (2 Tim. 1:5).

Early in 2 Timothy, Paul praises both Timothy's grandmother and mother, Lois and Eunice, respectively. These women were both converted Jews, although we know that Timothy's father was of Greek heritage. In this early Christian age, Timothy, who is said to have been converted himself circa A.D. 48, was actually a third-generation Christian. Not in the strict sense companions of Paul, his specific remembrance of them infers his admiration for the way in which Timothy was raised and for the profound effect their efforts had on behalf of his own ministry.

In both the Jewish and Greek cultures, women were similarly regarded—home *had* to be where the heart was. There was no other choice if a woman was to remain a respected part of the community. And so when Paul writes of Timothy's "sincere faith," we know that he is referring to two extraordinary women who ventured outside of their natural cultural heritage and courageously trained up Timothy in the way he should go, despite the dissension around them. Most of us have at least been on either the receiving or giving end of such glorious nurturing, and Paul, by his early acknowledgement of the origins of Timothy's faith, recognizes the transcendent virtue therein.

Dear God,
We needn't be mothers or grandmothers to involve
ourselves in the fate of a child. Even as these
women of the Bible—Mary and Elizabeth and Eunice
and Lois—set luminous ideals for us, help us
to remember that, through the quality of our teaching
and listening and, simply, in the way we live our lives,
we are passing along the golden standard of Christianity
that will be reflected in the ages to come.
Give us strength, insight, and heart and then
infect us with all manner of possibilities to do
exactly what it is You would have us do as the gift
of childhood innocence matures. Amen.

Timothy

I have no one like him who will be genuinely concerned for your welfare. All of them are seeking their own interests, not those of Jesus Christ. But Timothy's worth you know, how like a son with a father he has served with me in the work of the gospel (Phil. 2:20–22).

Here is Paul writing about Timothy, who somehow overcame his shyness and helped to build the foundations of several of the early churches, particularly at Corinth and Ephesus. Perhaps Paul had learned from his experience of discharging John Mark that youth has its own worthwhile expression and should be nurtured with very fine tuning. The record reveals that Timothy became Paul's "beloved son."

Of mixed Greek-Jewish heritage, Timothy was probably among the crowds who heard Paul when he made his first missionary journey, for it was on Paul's second journey that he was called to accompany him, along with Silas. Timothy seemed especially adept at helping struggling churches through difficult periods, for Paul often assigned him these duties. Although he was not always successful, Timothy's faithfulness could be counted upon. Paul's pastoral letters to him are timeless replicas of love, expressing all of the intensity so characteristic of Paul, even as he aged. Although the authorship of the two epistles of Timothy has been questioned by scholars over time, Paul's love for Timothy and Timothy's faithfulness to Paul require no speculation whatsoever!

Dear God,
Much can be learned from this reciprocal friendship.
The encouragement of youth included in our circle
of friends helps keep our eyes focused away from
our own maturing centeredness. Continuing education
means that we learn from, as well as listen to,
friends ready to accept both that which has been
successful for them, and that which has not.
Youthful zest might even be that powerful
paradigm we have been searching for. Amen.

Silas

Through Silvanus, whom I consider a faithful brother, I have written this short letter to encourage you and to testify that this is the true grace of God. Stand fast in it (1 Pet. 5:12).

*P*eter, in writing his final greetings in this beautiful first epistle, distinguishes Silas (also known as Silvanus) as his "faithful brother." Indeed, he was. Listen to his accomplishments, for God could not have provided a more steadfast friend than Silas, for he was one who shared his life with both Peter and Paul.

Involved in the earliest church decisions, he was among those who bore the important responsibility of being sent to carry the news to the Council of Jerusalem that the door of the church would be open to the Gentiles. He not only took Barnabas' place on Paul's second missionary journey, but he was the one who was jailed with Paul. Not wasting a moment's time while incarcerated, the two proceeded to convert their jailer!

Some scholars believe that Silas might even have been the author of 1 Peter, for he was Paul's as well as Peter's *amanuensis*, the one who received dictation from another. Known as "eloquent," this possibility is real, for Silas, while assisting Paul in a number of ways, is also thought to have cared for Peter before his martyrdom. He, therefore, would be one able to synchronize their thoughts into what became the beautiful and cohesive first epistle of Peter.

Dear God,
Here is a person who in many ways perhaps
reminds us of a family member or friend who seems
to be a kind of designated angel, able somehow
to share our times of overwhelming joy as well as
intense sorrow. Maybe they have been more
like a chorus of angels, but their earthly presence
has made us know that You have touched their hearts
and that their actions bespeak Your eternal care.
They make our lives worthwhile. Amen.

Christ the King
Christ the King Roman Catholic Church, Philadelphia, Pennsylvania

The Revelation of John

A few summers ago, I read William Barclay's study of Revelation. I did not especially enjoy reading it; neither could I put it down. Not easy to understand nor comforting, it can be read on many levels. I decided I would just relax and let it take its own course in my heart.

It occurred to me that I should share it with you. Revelation contains seven letters to seven churches in Asia: Ephesus, Smyrna, Pergamum, Thyatira, Sardis, Philadelphia, and Laodicea. Cosmopolitan they were! John begins his letter to each church by referring to them as the Seven Golden Lampstands; the seven stars are the leaders of the churches, and the one who walks among them is, of course, Jesus. The number seven is of symbolic importance; it was "the symbol of divine perfection."

Most authorities believe the author of Revelation was *not* John the apostle, but rather John the prophet, writing while in exile on the island of Patmos in the Aegean Sea. Revelation points out individual shortcomings of each church, while admonishing them to live more Christian lives. This was a time of the early growth of the church, as well as a time of severe persecution of Christians. There were many roads to misery one could travel—crime, immorality, loss of faith—all those things so terribly familiar to us today.

Although Revelation is often associated with the dread of Apocalypse, we would be better served to remember that its ultimate message was not one of doom and gloom, but rather renewal of personal faith within each church. Someone said that Revelation contains as many mysteries as it does words. Without getting bogged down in the details, read Revelation if you have not done so.

John begins with Ephesus, the same Ephesus to which Paul wrote and where Timothy became the first bishop of the church.

Ephesus

"I know your works, your toil and your patient endurance . . . but I have this against you—that you have left your first love" (Rev. 2:2).

Ephesus was the capital of Asia Minor, the highway to Rome. It was one of the wealthiest and greatest cities in all of Asia. It was a free, self-governing city—unusual across the vast lands of the Roman Empire—and was ranked alongside Alexandria in Egypt for its busy harbor. Paul established the church there in A.D. 53 when he was returning to Jerusalem. Paul addressed the Ephesians as "saints" in his first letter to them.

But pagan religion was also at its most powerful here; Ephesus was a center of immorality. The church at Ephesus had steadfastly refused to tolerate sin among its members, not easy in a city which was noted for its devious sexual practices. John first commends them for working hard at helping the community, while resisting sin. He recalls that, in their beginnings, they may not have had much knowledge, but love was the tapestry which bound them together.

By this time, however, the church at Ephesus was a second-generation church. Now the reverse was true. They were diminishing their faith in a most common way. John reminds them of the great rewards of following Jesus by believing, persevering, remaining faithful, and living as one who follows Christ. Then, he says, the tree of life will be theirs—the promise of paradise and eternal life.

Dear God,
You are the tree of all life. Without Your presence—
and, admittedly, in massive doses—our lives are
arid streams, suffering from exposure to the wrong
elements. We have only to turn our face toward
You to know what the possibilities of the promise of
paradise could mean. Would that we would not
waste a moment finding it within ourselves
to make that commitment. Amen.

Smyrna

"I know your affliction and your poverty, even though you are rich. I know the slander on the part of those who say that they are Jews and are not, but are a synagogue of Satan. Do not fear what you are about to suffer. Beware, the devil is about to throw some of you into prison so that you may be tested . . . Be faithful until death, and I will give you the crown of life" (Rev. 2:9–10).

There is a different tone in John's second letter to the Christians here. While in every letter he encouraged and praised, he always identified a characteristic which was corrupting. For the congregation at Smyrna, he only sympathized. He wanted them to understand that while they were currently suffering, a crown of victory was waiting for them in another place.

Why was there so much suffering in Smyrna? Called the "Ornament of Asia," it was a beautiful port city with wonderful views of land and sea. They even minted their own coins. What, then, was the source of their affliction? The Christians of Smyrna were allowed no space; the Jews would not let them worship. Those who weren't Jewish praised the Roman emperor, which was another form of worship in those times. John recognized that although they were materially poor, they were spiritually rich. He promised them that their suffering would garner for them a crown.

Dear God,

Everyone of us knows the varieties of pain which bring suffering. There is mental and emotional pain which can make us desperate; physical pain which can drive us from You, if we open ourselves to it; and the pain of uncertainty, which can dim our minds. Always remind us of our Christian heritage and the knowledge it brings that if we are at one with You, our suffering is eased and made bearable. In fact, we know that nothing is tolerable without You. You have promised us a crown; would that we would earn it in a most natural way. Amen.

Pergamum

"I know where you are living, where Satan's throne is. Yet you are holding fast to my name, and you did not deny your faith in me even in the days of Antipas my witness, my faithful one, who was killed among you . . . But I have a few things against you: you have some there who hold to the teaching of Balaam . . ." (Rev. 2:13–14).

Pergamum has been called the most "illustrious" city in Asia. Its public buildings were built in steep places. It was a beautiful Greek city, and recorded as being "a magnificent example of Hellenistic city planning." It possessed a paralleling magnificent culture; its library was considered second only to the great library at Alexandria. The Christians there were exceptionally faithful; yet they were exposed to efforts to teach them to live a life of conformity and, even worse, to worship the Roman emperor as if he were divine.

Barclay wastes not a breath in declaring that, "The man who is not prepared to be different need not start on the Christian way at all." So much for Christians and conformity! A group there known as the Nicolaitans, bent on teaching this vague approach to life, sought to inflict it on the Christians at Pergamum. As often is the case, some followed. But for those who remained faithful, there was promised a new name. The author of Revelation wrote: ". . . and I will give a white stone, and on the white stone is written a new name that no one knows except the one who receives it."

Dear God,

Would that the only status we cared about was our status with You. We need to consider this carefully, because when we think about it, this kind of reflection could bring us into the closest state of mind and heart we could possibly have. We sometimes care too much about what others think about us. And why? We know that You are all that matters and that, in the end, we save ourselves relentless sorrow when we recognize that we are drifting from that which we hold most dear. Come into our hearts, Lord Jesus. Be that about which we care the most, now and forever. Amen.

Thyatira

"I know your works, your love, service and patient endurance. . . . But I have this against you: you tolerate that woman Jezebel who . . . is teaching and beguiling my servants to practice fornication and to eat food sacrificed to idols. But to the rest of you. . . . who do not hold this teaching, who have not learned what some call the 'deep things of Satan,' . . . to you I say, I do not lay on you any other burden; only hold fast to what you have until I come. . . . I will also give the morning star" (Rev. 2:19–20, 20–25, 28).

John's longest letter is addressed to the church at Thyatira, another key commercial city. It was known for its guilds for people of different trades; i.e. wool, linens, potters, and craftsmen who worked with leather and metal. The Christians were not members of these guilds, because often their meetings would end with drinking and "slack morality."

John praises the church at Thyatira for its love and endurance. But cohabiting the church was the evil Jezebel, who tried her best to influence their behavior. She pled for compromise with the world's standards in the interests of business and commercial prosperity, assuring them without doubt that the Holy Spirit "would preserve them from harm." Not wishing to destroy the church, but rather to bring it into new ways which were destructive to the faith, she impaired its existence, by leading them to the "deep things of Satan." She has had a very long life.

Dear God,
Let us first put aside our day's study and remember
those who are ill. Restore life and lift the spirits
of those with special needs, dear God, according
to Your will. We remember special people
in our hearts at this moment.

How like the early Christians we are!
Compromise and toleration, accommodation
and adjustment, are easy to do and make.
Going along with the crowd, even when our conscience
pleads otherwise, is a path we have all taken.
Our humanity implies that we will stray at times,
but Your divinity, we know, will always bring us
back into the arms of uncompromising serenity.
Oh to be a morning star! Amen.

Sardis

*"I know thy works; you have a name of being alive, but you are dead.
Wake up, and strengthen what remains and is on the point of death, for I
have not found your works perfect in the sight of my God. Yet you still
have a few persons in Sardis who have not soiled their clothes; they will
walk with me, dressed in white, for they are worthy. If you conquer . . . I
will not blot your name out of the book of life . . ." (Rev. 3:1–5).*

Have you guessed Sardis' affliction? Here was a church
that appeared spotless on the outside. However, its
problem was one of degeneration and compromise, for there
was considerable wealth there, and John is chiding them for
what became their sheer indifference to the Christian way
of life.

True enough, it was probably difficult to establish a
church in Sardis, for many pagan cults flourished there,
many of them claiming to "restore life to the dead," an
appealing promise over the ages.

Recent excavations in Sardis revealed a "basilica that was
transformed into a synagogue" around A.D. 3. Scholars have
reasoned that certain conflict existed there between the
Jewish community and the still-young Christian church.
However, by the fourth century, a large basilica was built,
persuading us to believe that the church in Sardis had
regained its vitality.

Dear God,
When we consider the problem of degeneration
and its causes, we realize we must ever renew
our faith by everyday prayer and frequent study.
We need to reach not only out, but also reach
into ourselves, if we can ever hope to overcome
our own personal vulnerabilities.

Every day we need to say—Renew me, O Lord.
Drench me in the waters of your pure spirit.
May my even trying to live an unequivocally
Christian life be a naturally elegant necessity
for me. Perhaps, then, one day my name will be
included in Your Book of Life. Amen.

Philadelphia

"I know your works. Look, I have set before you an open door, which no one is able to shut. I know that you have little power, and yet you have kept my word and have not denied my name. Because you have kept my word of patient endurance, I will keep you from the hour of trial that is coming on the whole world to test the inhabitants of the earth" (Rev. 3:8–10).

Of Philadelphia we may fairly ask—what is in a name? The youngest of the seven cities, from John it received the greatest praise. It is named for someone who loved his brother so much that he was called *Philadelphos;* thus we know why Philadelphia is called the City of Brotherly Love.

Strategically located on the west between Sardis and Pergamum and Laodicea on the east, Philadelphia was founded by the king of Pergamum around 150 B.C. However, Philadelphia suffered from the same chaotic condition to which several of the other cities were subjected—inevitable conflict with the Jews. Philadelphia, unlike Sardis and Smyrna, flexed its Christian muscle and endured. For this they are promised an "open door," and exclusion from the "hour of trial" John prophesizes is coming. John is talking about a certain kind of Christian freedom few will experience. Eventually, every other city we have discussed fell to Mohammed beginning in the seventh century. Philadelphia remained faithful to its Christian calling—the last bastion of Christianity in Asia Minor. There still remains a Christian church although the city finally fell in the fourteenth century.

Dear God,

We pray that we may live our lives ever faithfully to our Christian beliefs and morals. This, we all know, is easier to do at certain times than at others. But in Jesus we have a model who has taught us enduring principles about how to live our lives even during the more demanding ebb and flow of what seems to be life's unwelcome twists. Remind us that the coveted characteristic of serenity, reflected by saints who have gone before us, can be ours when we faithfully follow our Christian calling. Amen.

Laodicea

"I know your works; you are neither cold nor hot. I wish that you were either cold or hot. So, because you are lukewarm, and neither cold nor hot, I am about to spit you out of my mouth. For you say, 'I am rich, I have prospered, and I need nothing.' . . . Listen! I am standing at the door, knocking; if you hear my voice and open the door, I will come in to you" (Rev. 3:15–17, 20).

Laodicea was founded in 250 B.C. and was yet another "distinguished and wealthy city." It was a financial, commercial, and medical center—so wealthy that it had grown impoverished spiritually, by now a familiar pattern among these early churches. For this abuse of wealth, Laodicea receives the worst condemnation of all. Being neither hot nor cold might seem a better state than being "degenerate" as was Sardis, or compromising, as was Pergamum, but Laodicea's indifference was something John found wholly repulsive. Even as John implores them to repent, it does not seem a possibility. We are left with an image of Christ knocking at the door of their hearts, not knowing if, indeed, that crimson door was ever opened.

Dear God,
Keep us from the worst of sins as recorded here—
that of indifference or fear to take a stand.
It can choke the heart and rob the soul. It can cut
us off from knowing the One genuine source of
light through which we can view the world
with a sense of security.

Give us the desire to look again—with renewed
intensity—at our own commitment to You. Let us
ask our hearts: Am I faithful? Do I care?
Do my prayers refresh me or leave me tepid?
Do You knock on a door which never quite opens
all the way? Revitalize each of us. Renew us with
a strength we can only have when we welcome You
with all the energy we possess. Amen.

Nativity
St. Thomas Episcopal Church, St. Petersburg, Florida